HERE AND NOW

The Art of Mindful Living

INNISAI ARANGANATHAN

Copyright © Innisai Aranganathan 2024
All Rights Reserved.

ISBN 979-8-89186-858-8

This book has been published with all efforts taken to make the material error-free after the consent of the author. However, the author and the publisher do not assume and hereby disclaim any liability to any party for any loss, damage, or disruption caused by errors or omissions, whether such errors or omissions result from negligence, accident, or any other cause.

While every effort has been made to avoid any mistake or omission, this publication is being sold on the condition and understanding that neither the author nor the publishers or printers would be liable in any manner to any person by reason of any mistake or omission in this publication or for any action taken or omitted to be taken or advice rendered or accepted on the basis of this work. For any defect in printing or binding the publishers will be liable only to replace the defective copy by another copy of this work then available.

Contents

CHAPTER - I

The Great Start

In the hustle and bustle of today's fast-paced, tech-infused world, it's alarmingly common to find ourselves teetering on the edge of overwhelming stress and an unsettling disconnect from both ourselves and the people around us.

Picture this: we're perpetually in motion, frantically hopping from one task to another, juggling and multitasking in a desperate attempt to stay afloat in the endless sea of tasks laid out before us. And, if that wasn't enough, it's as though we're tethered to our gadgets, persistently "on" and ensnared in a digital web that seems impossible to escape.

But hold on a moment, because amidst this maddening confusion, there exists a profound and transformative remedy — mindfulness. It's not merely a passing trend but rather an ancient practice, as timeless as the flowing rivers and steadfast mountains. Mindfulness, in essence, is the art of bringing our consciousness into the immediate present, sans any harsh judgment or distracting detours.

It entails attuning ourselves to the symphony of our thoughts, emotions, and physical sensations, nurturing a deep sense of curiosity, and fostering an open-hearted acceptance of every experience that washes over us.

Imagine it as the pause button in our ceaseless race against time, the antidote to our perpetual state of distraction, and the key to unlocking a world of profound self-awareness and inner peace.

The Essence of Mindfulness

Mindfulness isn't just a passing fancy, akin to those eye-catching neon legwarmers that defined the fashion scene of the '80s. No, it is a wisdom as enduring as the tales of Grandma's cherished cookie recipe – though, truth be told, the benefits of mindfulness might just outshine even those delicious cookies. This practice finds its roots in the profound wellspring of ancient Eastern spiritual traditions, such as Buddhism and Hinduism.

Picture this: serene monks in the heart of tranquil monasteries, their spirits calm as still waters, while we in the modern world, flustered and exasperated, engage in epic quests to locate our elusive TV remote controls.

But wait, there's a twist! Mindfulness has evolved and expanded far beyond its original Eastern confines. It has transformed into a universal phenomenon, as ubiquitous as the lamentable quality of airport coffee. This isn't merely about escaping the monotonous routines of life or, as some might jest, "practicing zen while watching paint dry." No, it's a profound endeavor that beckons you to awaken fully to each passing moment, akin to a curious cat convinced that a humble cardboard box is the doorway to an alternate universe.

The Mindful Journey

Now, as you embark on this journey into the realm of mindfulness, you might be pondering, "Alright, mindfulness, but how does it benefit me?" Well, dear reader, prepare yourself for a veritable feast of mindfulness offerings. In the pages of this book, we are about to lay out a sumptuous banquet of mindfulness, rich and diverse, much like a menu at a five-star restaurant.

We won't merely touch the basics; no, we shall dive deep into the depths of this practice, uncovering its hidden gems and offering you the equivalent of gourmet dishes for your mind and soul. But it doesn't stop there; we will also guide you in sprinkling the essence of mindfulness onto the canvas of your relationships, your workplace, and your personal growth, much like a cosmic seasoning that adds an unparalleled zest to life.

But let's not forget the key ingredient – balance. We won't inundate you with dry, academic jargon. Instead, we aim to strike a harmonious equilibrium. We'll infuse a hint of scientific research, akin to a subtle seasoning that enhances the flavor, a pinch of personal anecdotes, like the secret ingredient passed down through generations, and a generous handful of practical exercises, much like a recipe that turns raw ingredients into a delectable dish. In essence, we're your culinary guides on this tantalizing journey towards a better, more mindful life.

The Mindful Voyage Begins

Now, as you stand at the precipice, primed and prepared to plunge headlong into the boundless depths of mindfulness, let us embark together on this audacious odyssey. Close your eyes and conjure this vivid imagery: you find yourself standing at the very cusp of a colossal sea, a sea of mindfulness, stretching infinitely before you. Your mind, my dear friend, is your vessel, your trusted ship on this remarkable voyage. For far too long, it has sailed these waters on autopilot, navigating the tides of habit and routine without a captain at the helm.

But today marks a new chapter in your journey. Today, you seize the helm with a determined hand, ready to steer your ship through uncharted waters.

The Art of Mindfulness

Imagine your mind is a caffeine-fueled monkey, leaping from thought to thought at a speed that would put a hummingbird to shame. It's like trying to say "banana" as quickly as you can, except your thoughts are even faster. It's a whirlwind up there, a storm of ideas, memories, worries, and daydreams.

Now, let's talk about the first step in mindfulness. It's a bit like that moment when you're already in the bathroom, and you suddenly realize you forgot to buy toilet paper. You're standing there, contemplating your next move, and it dawns on you that it's a little late to do anything about it. But, hey, at least you've become aware of the situation.

That's the essence of mindfulness – becoming aware of the chaotic monkey-mind that's been running the show. It's about recognizing that your thoughts are racing around like that hyperactive monkey, and it's time to take charge.

But here's where it gets interesting. Mindfulness doesn't tell you to wrestle those thoughts to the ground and tie them up. No, it's more like tuning into your very own mental sitcom. You're the audience, and your thoughts are the stars of the show. They prance onto the stage, do their thing, and then exit, stage left.

You get to sit back with a metaphorical bucket of popcorn and watch the whole spectacle. Sometimes it's a comedy, with thoughts that make you laugh out loud. Other times, it's a drama, with thoughts that tug at your heartstrings.

The key is this: you're not getting caught up in the plot. You're not the director trying to script the perfect scene, and you're certainly not the lead actor trying to control every moment. You're the audience, observing with curiosity and without judgment.

Here's a practical example. Imagine you're sitting in a meeting at work, and suddenly a thought pops into your head: "Did I leave the oven on at home?" In the past, you might have let that thought hijack your attention. You'd start worrying, picturing your house in flames, and mentally berating yourself for being so forgetful.

But with mindfulness, you're the audience. You notice the thought: "Did I leave the oven on?" You don't try to answer it or follow it down a rabbit hole of anxiety. Instead, you acknowledge it, maybe even smile at the quirkiness of your mind, and then gently bring your focus back to the meeting.

In this way, mindfulness is like a remote control for your mental TV. You can switch channels, change the volume, or even turn it off when you need a break. You're no longer at the mercy of the monkey-mind; you're the one holding the remote.

So, the next time your mind goes into hyperdrive, remember the caffeine-fueled monkey and the sitcom in your head. Take a seat in the audience, grab your popcorn, and enjoy the show. Mindfulness isn't about getting rid of your thoughts; it's about changing your relationship with them. And in doing so, you just might find a sense of peace and clarity you never knew was possible.

The Power of Presence

The enchantment of mindfulness lies not in the art of emptying one's mind or suppressing the ceaseless parade of thoughts. It resides in the profound joy of immersing oneself in the splendid chaos of the present moment. Imagine, for a moment, savoring a cheeseburger with the same reverence you might afford a gourmet meal at a five-star restaurant. Envision the sensation of the sun's warm embrace on your skin, transporting you to a far-off tropical paradise. Picture yourself engaged in rapt attention as your friend regales you with their epic dating saga, your mind unburdened by the mental checklist of groceries.

This state of presence isn't a mere parlor trick, nor is it an inconsequential change. It's a transformative force, capable of turning mundane moments into extraordinary ones. It's the alchemy that can transmute chaos into order, and assemble the scattered pieces of your life into a breathtaking masterpiece.

Consider this book your golden ticket to the wild rollercoaster ride of mindfulness. Whether you're a novice setting foot on this intriguing path or a seasoned traveler with miles underfoot, we've reserved a seat just for you. By the final chapter, you'll not only possess a well-stocked toolbox of mindfulness techniques but also a wealth of knowledge to craft a profound transformation in your life.

So, my dear reader, it's time to set aside the constant companion that is your smartphone, if only for a moment. Take a deep, refreshing breath, for you're about to embark on an exhilarating and often humorous journey into the realm of mindfulness. It's a quest to unplug your mind from the distractions of modern life and reawaken to the vibrant tapestry of existence itself. Welcome aboard!

What is mindfulness?

Welcome to the delightful journey into the whimsical world of mindfulness, where being present is the name of the game, and judgments are left at the door – just like an exclusive club for the here and now.

So, what exactly is this mindfulness thing, you ask? Well, think of it as the art of living in the moment, like savoring the last piece of chocolate cake without worrying about the calories. It's about being fully engaged with whatever is happening right here, right now, without your mind playing hopscotch between the past and future.

But hold onto your hats, folks, because it's not as easy as it sounds. Our minds are like overeager puppies, constantly chasing after thoughts, emotions, and every shiny distraction in sight. It's a real circus up there.

Picture this: you're trying to have a peaceful moment, perhaps enjoying a cup of tea. Suddenly, your mind goes, "Hey, remember that embarrassing thing you did five years ago?" And just like that, you're catapulted back in time, cringing at your past self. Or maybe it goes, "What if you fail that big presentation next week?" Now you're on a rollercoaster of anxiety, clutching your tea like it's a lifeline.

But fear not, for mindfulness is your trusty sidekick in this chaotic mind-circus. It's like having a front-row seat to the show without getting entangled in the acrobatics. You watch those thoughts and feelings tumble and somersault without passing judgment, just as you'd observe a quirky street performance.

Eckhart Tolle, a renowned spiritual teacher and author, offers a profound reflection: "Realize deeply that the present moment is all you ever have. Make the Now the primary focus of your life."

So, why bother with all this mindfulness business? Well, think of it as a mental upgrade, like trading in your rusty old bicycle for a sleek, turbocharged spaceship. It's about understanding your thoughts and emotions, seeing the patterns in your behavior, and connecting the dots in your relationships.

Imagine having the superpower to pause before reacting to a pesky email from your boss or a snarky comment from your neighbor. You'd become a Jedi of self-control, a Zen master of inner peace. That's what mindfulness can do for you.

So, my fellow explorer of the present moment, get ready for an adventure that's both enlightening and, dare I say, a tad amusing. In the pages that follow, we'll unravel the mysteries of mindfulness with stories, quotes, and practical exercises that will tickle your curiosity and light the path to inner serenity. Grab your mental safari hat and join us as we embark on this journey into the whimsical world of mindfulness.

Benefits of mindfulness

Ah, mindfulness, the buzzword of the century. It's been making waves lately, like the latest viral meme. But hey, there's more to it than just a passing trend. It's a bit like that trusty old Swiss army knife — versatile, practical, and jam-packed with benefits.

Let's dive into this world of mindfulness, where being present is the name of the game. You see, it's not about emptying your mind or suppressing those thoughts that pop up like unsolicited ads. Nope, it's about embracing the glorious mess of the present moment. It's about savoring life's cheeseburgers as if they were five-star gourmet meals, feeling the sun's warm caress on your skin as if you're on a tropical vacation, and actually listening to your friend's epic dating saga without mentally drafting your grocery list.

Now, you might wonder, what's the big deal? Well, let's break it down, shall we? First off, mindfulness is like a stress-reduction ninja. It helps you kick stress to the curb and promotes relaxation. Picture this: you're in the middle of a chaotic workday, deadlines looming like thunderclouds. Instead of panicking, mindfulness swoops in and whispers, "Hey, let's take a breather." It's like having a personal zen coach in your corner.

Here's a related quote by *Eckhart Tolle*, a spiritual teacher and author: "The primary cause of unhappiness is never the situation but your thoughts about it. Be aware of the thoughts you are thinking. Separate them from the situation, which is always neutral, which always is as it is."

But that's not all. Mindfulness isn't just about you and your inner calm. It's a social butterfly, too. By sprinkling a little mindfulness magic into your interactions with others, you can build deeper connections and communicate like a pro. Imagine this: you're chatting with a colleague, and instead of mentally rehearsing your grocery list (again), you're fully present. You hear their words, see their expressions, and boom – you're connecting on a whole new level. It's like discovering a secret superpower in your social toolkit.

Now, hold on to your hats because here's where it gets juicy – the physical perks. Research shows that mindfulness can lower blood pressure, ease chronic pain, and even tuck you in for a night of better sleep. It's like a spa day for your body and mind rolled into one.

But wait, there's more! Mindfulness doesn't just stop at stress-busting and physical wellness. It's your secret weapon for boosting creativity and productivity. Imagine you're at work, drowning in a sea of emails and to-do lists. Mindfulness taps you on the shoulder and says, "Let's focus, buddy." Suddenly, your ideas flow like a river, and problems become puzzles waiting to be solved. It's like having a mental superhero cape tucked in your desk drawer.

Now, before you get too carried away, remember that mindfulness isn't a quick fix. It's not a magic wand you wave once and ta-da, you're Zen

Master Supreme. Nope, it's a lifelong practice, a bit like learning to dance. It takes patience, persistence, and the ability to laugh at your two left feet.

Mindfulness is a powerful practice that can offer a wide range of benefits for those who practice it regularly. Whether you are looking to improve your mental health, enhance your physical well-being, or cultivate a more compassionate and fulfilling approach to life, mindfulness can be a valuable tool for achieving your goals. Here are some of the major benefits that practicing mindfulness can provide you:

- **Reduced stress and anxiety**: Mindfulness is like a mental tool that can help you deal with stress and anxiety better. It works by making you more aware of your thoughts and emotions. When you're mindful, you notice when you're feeling stressed or anxious, and you don't react right away. Instead, you take a moment to understand what's going on in your mind, and this helps you respond to these feelings in a calm and balanced manner. It's like having a pause button for your stress and anxiety, giving you the chance to choose how you want to react.

- **Improved mental health**: Practicing mindfulness regularly can make you feel better if you're struggling with feelings of sadness or nervousness. It's like a workout for your mind that helps improve your mental well-being. Studies have even shown that it can help reduce symptoms of depression and anxiety. So, it's like a mental exercise that can lead to a happier and healthier mind.

- **Better physical health**: Mindfulness isn't just good for your mind; it's good for your body too! People who practice mindfulness regularly have seen some cool physical benefits. It can help to lower your blood pressure, which is good for your heart. It also reduces inflammation in your body, which can make you feel better overall. Plus, it can even improve your sleep, so you wake up feeling more refreshed and ready to take on the day! So, it's like a double win for your mind and body.

- **Increased focus and attention**: Mindfulness is like a workout for your mind! When you practice mindfulness, you're training your mind to stay focused on what's happening right now. This can be super helpful for improving your concentration and staying engaged in tasks. So, if you ever find yourself easily distracted or having a hard time staying on track with your work or studies, mindfulness can be your secret weapon to boost your focus and productivity. It's like giving your brain a little exercise to make it stronger and more attentive!

- **Increased resilience**: Think of mindfulness as your emotional superhero cape! When you practice mindfulness, you're like a superhero in training, building your emotional resilience. This means you become better at handling tough situations and bouncing back when life throws you a curveball. Imagine you're playing a video game. At first, you might not be very good, and you get knocked down a lot. But with practice, you learn to dodge obstacles, overcome challenges, and keep going no matter what. That's what mindfulness does for your emotions. It helps you dodge those emotional punches and come back even stronger. So, when life gets tough and you feel like you're in a video game, remember that mindfulness is your power-up, giving you the strength to face whatever comes your way!.

- **Enhanced self-awareness**: Imagine having a friendly, understanding friend inside your head. That's what mindfulness helps you become – your own best friend! You know how sometimes you can be really hard on yourself? Like when you make a mistake and you keep thinking about it, making yourself feel bad? Mindfulness is like having a kind friend who says, "Hey, it's okay. We all make mistakes. Let's learn from it and move on." With mindfulness, you start noticing your thoughts and feelings without judging yourself. It's like you're watching clouds in the sky – you see them, but you don't say, "That cloud is bad" or "That cloud is good." You just watch them come and go. So, mindfulness helps you treat yourself with kindness and understanding, like you would with a good friend. It's like giving yourself a warm, comforting hug from the inside!

- **Improved relationships**: Think about how sometimes you might not really listen when someone talks to you. Your mind might be thinking about other things or planning what to say next. It happens to all of us! Mindfulness helps you become a better listener and communicator. When you practice it, you become really good at paying attention to the person you're talking to. You're not thinking about what to say next or getting distracted by other thoughts. You're fully there, with them, in the moment. And when you're like that, people notice! They feel like you truly care about what they're saying, and that makes your relationships better. It's like you're sending them a message: "I'm here for you. I'm listening, and I care." So, mindfulness helps you become a fantastic communicator and have better relationships with others. It's like being a great friend to everyone you meet!

- **Increased creativity**: Imagine you're trying to solve a puzzle, but your mind keeps wandering. You're thinking about what to have for dinner or something you need to do tomorrow. It's tough to focus on the puzzle, right? Mindfulness is like a mental superpower for creativity. When you practice it, you become really good at staying focused on what you're doing right now. So, when you're working on a creative project, your mind doesn't wander off. It's right there, fully engaged. This laser-like focus helps you come up with new and exciting ideas. You can connect the dots that others might miss because your mind is clear and open to inspiration. It's like having a creativity booster in your brain! So, mindfulness is not just about being calm; it's about unlocking your creative genius. It helps you stay in the moment and let those brilliant ideas flow. Who knows what amazing things you'll create with mindfulness by your side!

- **Improved decision-making**: Imagine you're in a candy store, and there are so many delicious treats to choose from. Your emotions are saying, "I want all of them!" It's easy to get carried away and make decisions based on your cravings. Mindfulness is like having a wise friend with you. It reminds you to pause and think. Instead of acting on impulse, you take a moment to breathe and consider your choices. By staying in the present moment, you can make decisions that align with your goals and values. You're less likely to be swayed by fleeting emotions or external distractions. It's like having a compass that guides you in the right direction. So, mindfulness helps you make choices that you won't regret later..

- **Increased emotional regulation**: Imagine your emotions are like waves in the ocean. Sometimes, they're gentle, and other times, they're big and turbulent. When those big waves come, it's easy to get carried away and feel overwhelmed. Mindfulness is like learning to surf. Instead of getting knocked over by those powerful waves, you learn to ride them. You become aware of your emotions without judgment, which means you don't criticize yourself for feeling a certain way. By acknowledging your emotions and accepting them as a natural part of life, you gain better control over them. You can decide how to respond to those emotions instead of reacting impulsively. It's like having a superpower to stay calm in the middle of life's emotional storms. So, mindfulness helps you manage your feelings and avoid getting stuck in negative thoughts. It's like having an emotional safety net that keeps you steady when things get tough.

- **Greater sense of purpose**: Think of mindfulness as a treasure map for your inner self. You know, like those old maps with an "X" that marks the spot where the treasure is hidden. Well, in this case, the treasure isn't gold or jewels; it's your values and purpose in life. Sometimes, we get so caught up in the busyness of life that we forget what truly matters to us. Mindfulness is like a magnifying glass that helps you see those values more clearly. It's a reminder of what's important to you, like spending time with loved ones, being kind, or pursuing your passions. When you practice mindfulness, you're taking a moment to check your map and make sure you're heading in the right direction. It helps you connect with your inner compass, so you can find more meaning and fulfillment on your life's journey. It's like rediscovering your own personal treasure every day.

- **Enhanced creativity**: Imagine your mind is a garden, and creativity is the beautiful flowers that grow there. But sometimes, weeds of doubt, routine, or overthinking can crowd out those creative blossoms. Now, mindfulness is like a gentle gardener. It comes in and helps clear away those weeds. How? By making you more open and curious. When you're curious, it's like planting new seeds in your mental garden. You start asking questions, exploring ideas, and seeing things from different angles. This curiosity helps your creative flowers bloom brighter and more often. Mindfulness encourages you to embrace the moment, to be present and attentive. And when you do, you might find inspiration in the smallest details – a sunset, a conversation, or a simple object. It's like finding hidden treasures in your own backyard. So, by nurturing curiosity through mindfulness, you can create a garden of creativity that's always in full bloom, ready to inspire you in all areas of life.

- **Improved communication**: Imagine you have a superpower - the ability to truly understand what others are thinking and feeling. That's empathy, and mindfulness can help you unlock it. When you practice mindfulness, you become more aware of your own thoughts and feelings. But it doesn't stop there; it also makes you more sensitive to the thoughts and feelings of those around you. It's like putting on someone else's shoes and walking in them for a while. You start to see the world from their perspective. This helps you understand them better and connect on a deeper level. In personal relationships, empathy can lead to more meaningful conversations and a stronger bond with your loved ones. At work, it can make you a better team player and leader because you can relate to your colleagues' experiences and concerns. So, with mindfulness as your ally, you can tap into your empathetic superpower and build richer, more fulfilling relationships with the people in your life.

- **Greater self-compassion**: Imagine you have a little voice in your head that's always criticizing you, pointing out your flaws, and making you feel bad about yourself. That voice can be pretty harsh, right? Well, mindfulness is like a friendly companion who helps you quiet that critical voice. When you practice mindfulness, you learn to be kinder to yourself, like a best friend offering comfort and understanding. Instead of beating yourself up for mistakes or feeling inadequate, you start accepting yourself just as you are, flaws and all. This self-compassion can be incredibly healing. It's like giving yourself a warm, comforting hug from the inside. When you're kinder to yourself, you become more resilient and better equipped to handle life's challenges. You don't let setbacks or failures define your self-worth. You treat yourself with the same care and understanding you'd offer to a dear friend. So, with mindfulness by your side, you can cultivate self-compassion and live a happier, more content life, free from the burden of self-criticism and doubt.

- **Increased gratitude**: Imagine you have a magical pair of glasses, and when you put them on, you see the world in a whole new way. You notice the colors are brighter, the sounds are clearer, and the little everyday things become like small miracles. Well, mindfulness is like those magical glasses for your mind. When you practice mindfulness, it's as if you're putting on those glasses and seeing the world with fresh eyes. You start to notice the beauty in simple things – the warmth of the sun on your skin, the sound of birds singing, the taste of your favorite food. Even the ordinary moments become extraordinary. This newfound appreciation fills your heart with gratitude. You start feeling thankful for the little joys in life – a smile from a friend, a kind word, or a moment of peace. Gratitude becomes your companion, and it brings a sense of contentment and happiness. You realize that there's so much to be thankful for, even in the midst of life's challenges. So, with mindfulness, you can wear those magical glasses for your mind and see the world as a place full of wonders, leading to a life filled with gratitude and appreciation.

- **Improved physical performance**: Think of your favorite athlete, the one who always seems calm under pressure, making incredible plays or winning races effortlessly. Have you ever wondered how they do it? Well, one of their secrets might be mindfulness. Mindfulness is like a superpower for athletes. It helps them stay focused, calm, and perform at their best, even in high-pressure situations like important games or competitions. Imagine you're a basketball player about to take a crucial free throw in the final seconds of a game. The crowd is roaring, and the outcome rests on your shoulders. Without mindfulness, you might feel overwhelmed, your thoughts racing with doubts and worries. But if you've trained in mindfulness, you can take a deep breath, center yourself, and block out the distractions. You're in the present moment, fully focused on that free throw. Your body and mind are working together harmoniously. The same applies to other sports and physical activities. Whether you're a runner, a swimmer, a gymnast, or a weightlifter, mindfulness can improve your performance. It helps you handle pressure, stay in the zone, and achieve your personal best. So, next time you watch your favorite athlete, remember that behind their extraordinary feats, there might be a mindful mind at work, helping them shine in the spotlight. And who knows, with a little mindfulness practice, you could enhance your own physical performance too!

Alright, picture this: You're in a big, colorful circus, and the circus is all about mindfulness. Maybe you've never been to this circus before, or perhaps you've been here a few times. Either way, we're your friendly circus guides. By the time you finish reading this book, you'll have a toolbox filled with cool mindfulness tricks that you can use in every part of your life. It's like having a treasure chest of mindfulness secrets. Imagine setting aside your smartphone for a moment, taking a nice, deep breath, and joining us on this fun and eye-opening journey into the world of mindfulness. It's like stepping away from all the distractions and really getting into the groove of life. Think of the benefits of mindfulness as endless, just like a never-ending bowl of your all-time favorite comfort food. So, are you ready to dive in and explore the wonderful world of mindfulness with us? It's going to be quite an adventure!

How mindfulness can improve mental and physical health?

In the whirlwind of modern life, where our schedules seem to resemble a never-ending marathon and distractions lurk around every corner, enter mindfulness like a sage, offering a transformative embrace for both our mental and physical well-being. It's not just another relaxation technique; it's an art, a way of life. So, dear reader, fasten your seatbelt as we embark on a journey that will reveal how mindfulness can be your trusty ally in the quest for holistic health.

- **Stress Reduction and Anxiety Management:** Mindfulness is like a superhero that helps people deal with stress and anxiety. How? Well, it's like this: When you're mindful, you pay super close attention to what's happening right now, in this very moment. You don't let your mind run off to the past or the future, where stress and anxiety often hang out. Imagine if stress and anxiety were like fire-breathing dragons. Instead of panicking when you see one, mindfulness helps you stay cool. It's like having a shield that protects you. With mindfulness, you can calmly observe your thoughts and feelings without letting them control you. You become the dragon-tamer! So, when stress and anxiety come knocking, mindfulness is your trusty sidekick, helping you stay aware and not react automatically. It's like having a secret weapon to keep those dragons at bay and find peace in the midst of chaos.
- **Emotional Regulation:** Normally, when you feel an emotion, you might react to it right away. For example, if you feel angry, you might shout or get upset. But with mindfulness, you become a calm and curious observer. You look into the mirror and say, "Oh, there's anger." You don't judge it as good or bad; you simply notice it. This nonjudgmental observation is like having a superpower. It allows you to see your emotions without getting carried away by them. It's as if you're watching a movie of your emotions, and you can decide how you want to respond. So, mindfulness helps you become the master of your emotions, rather than letting them

control you. It's like having a remote control for your feelings, and you get to choose how you want to react. It's a powerful tool for emotional well-being.

- **Improved Focus and Concentration:** Imagine your mind is like a butterfly, always fluttering from one flower to another. It's hard to get anything done when your mind is so busy and distracted, right? Now, picture mindfulness as a gentle hand guiding that butterfly to one beautiful flower and encouraging it to stay there. With mindfulness, you learn to focus your mind on what you're doing right now. When you're studying, for example, instead of thinking about what you'll have for dinner or worrying about a test, mindfulness helps you stay with your books. You become like a laser beam of concentration. This laser-like focus is super helpful. It means you can get your work done faster and better. You understand things more clearly because your mind isn't all over the place. So, mindfulness is like having a secret power that makes you super productive and smart!.

- **Enhanced Self-Awareness:** Imagine your mind is like a cozy room with lots of furniture, and your thoughts and emotions are like different pieces of furniture in that room. Sometimes, it can get a bit cluttered in there, right? Now, think of mindfulness as your inner decorator. It helps you arrange the furniture neatly and organize the room. With mindfulness, you start to understand each piece of furniture better, like where it came from and why it's there. This understanding makes you feel more at home in your own mind. You can be yourself without getting overwhelmed by all the thoughts and emotions. It's like decluttering your mental space and finding your true self underneath all the chaos. So, mindfulness is like having an inner interior designer for your mind, helping you grow and be the real you.

- **Reduced Rumination and Overthinking:** Imagine you have a friend who always talks too much about their problems and worries. They keep going in circles, repeating the same things over and over. It's exhausting, right? Now, think of your own mind sometimes doing the same thing—going over the same worries again and again. It's like your mind has a broken record playing the same tune. Mindfulness is like being a DJ for your mind. It helps you switch tracks when your mind gets stuck in that endless loop. With mindfulness, you can say, "Let's play a different song!" It stops the mental repetition. By doing this, you give your mind a break, like a breath of fresh air. You clear away the mental fog and see things more clearly. It's like turning off the broken record and enjoying the silence or a new, happier tune. So, mindfulness is like being a DJ for your mind, changing the mental playlist, and giving yourself a mental break.

- **Boosted Resilience and Coping Skills:** Imagine you're walking in a park, and suddenly, it starts raining. Instead of getting upset or running for cover, you decide to embrace the rain. You let the raindrops fall on your face, and you enjoy the feeling of being in the moment, even though it's unexpected. Mindfulness is a bit like that. It's about facing challenges and difficulties with an attitude of acceptance. Instead of resisting or fighting against them, you learn to acknowledge them and allow them to be a part of your experience. Just like enjoying the rain, mindfulness helps you embrace the ups and downs of life. When you accept things as they are, it doesn't mean you're giving up or being passive. It means you're approaching them with an open heart and mind, ready to learn and grow from the experience. So, mindfulness is like dancing in the rain of life, accepting whatever comes your way with grace and resilience.

- **Pain Management:** Imagine you have a headache, and it feels like a heavy weight on your head. Normally, it's quite bothersome, and you can't stop thinking about how much it hurts. But with mindfulness, you approach it differently. Instead of focusing all your attention on the pain and making it worse by worrying about it, mindfulness helps you step back a bit. You observe the pain without getting caught up in it. You might notice that it's not just a heavy weight, but there are other sensations – perhaps some throbbing or tension. By observing the pain in this way, you change how it feels. It becomes less overwhelming, and you're not as bothered by it. It's like taking the sharp edges off the pain. Mindfulness doesn't make the pain go away entirely, but it helps you manage it better. It's like having a superpower that lets you deal with discomfort in a calmer and more composed way.

- **Lowered Blood Pressure and Heart Health:** Let's talk about your heart – not the one that feels emotions, but the one that pumps blood in your body. Sometimes, this heart can have problems, like high blood pressure, which is like the pressure of water in a hose that's too strong. It's not good for your heart. Now, mindfulness comes to the rescue. It's like a gentle breeze that helps lower that high pressure. When you practice mindfulness, you become calmer, and your heart doesn't have to work as hard. It's like the breeze is soothing your heart, making it healthier. So, mindfulness isn't just good for your mind; it's also a friend to your heart. It keeps your blood pressure in check, and that's like giving your heart a big, relaxing hug.

- **Better Sleep Quality:** Imagine you're lying in your cozy bed, ready for a good night's sleep. But sometimes, your mind is like a busy bee, buzzing with thoughts and worries, making it hard to fall asleep. That's when mindfulness steps in, like a sleep superhero. When you practice mindfulness, you calm that buzzing bee. It's like a lullaby for your mind. Your thoughts slow down, and you start to relax. Your body feels like a soft cloud, and sleep becomes easier to find. So, mindfulness is your secret weapon for better sleep. It helps you drift off into dreamland and wake up feeling refreshed, like you've had the best sleep of your life.

- **Enhanced Mind-Body Connection:** Imagine your mind and body as best friends who are sometimes out of sync. Your mind might say, "Let's eat lots of ice cream!" while your body says, "No, that's not so good for us." Mindfulness brings them back together like a friendship reunion. It helps you listen to your body's signals better. When you're hungry, you eat but stop when you're full. You start making healthier choices because you're more in tune with what your body needs. It's like having a personal health advisor inside you, guiding you to make the right choices. With mindfulness, your mind and body become a harmonious team, working together for your well-being.

Imagine this: you're navigating the chaotic streets of a bustling city, your mind racing as if it's late for an important meeting. This is the reality of our lives, constantly bombarded by stressors and anxieties. Now, picture mindfulness as your serene oasis in the midst of this urban jungle. It's the pause button for your racing thoughts, the life vest in the sea of stress. With mindfulness, you learn to be present, to face stress head-on, and to respond with the grace of a seasoned diplomat. It's like having your own personal Zen master, teaching you the art of tranquility in the midst of chaos.

Joseph Goldstein, a prominent meditation teacher, shares a similar perspective: "We can't stop the waves, but we can learn to surf." With mindfulness, you're not fighting the waves of stress; you're riding them with elegance and balance.

But that's just the tip of the iceberg. Mindfulness isn't just about keeping stress at bay; it's your emotional superhero. Imagine you're in a heated argument with a friend, emotions running wild. Instead of hurling words you might later regret, mindfulness taps you on the shoulder and whispers, "Take a breath, my friend." It's like having an emotional reset button, allowing you to navigate the stormy seas of emotions with finesse.

Now, let's talk productivity. In our age of constant distractions, staying focused is like trying to juggle flaming torches on a tightrope. Enter mindfulness, your secret weapon for improved focus and concentration. Imagine you're at work, surrounded by a mountain of tasks. Instead of succumbing to the siren call of social media or daydreaming about your next vacation, mindfulness takes your hand and says, "Let's stay here, shall we?" It's like having a mental coach, helping you stay on track and boosting your productivity.

But wait, there's more. Mindfulness isn't just a tool for the mind; it's a mirror that reflects your inner self. It's like a backstage pass to your own thoughts and emotions. Through mindfulness, you develop a profound self-awareness, like finally understanding the mysterious workings of a complex machine.

Now, let's talk about the monkey mind – the relentless chatterbox in your head that replays past mistakes and rehearses future scenarios. Mindfulness is your mute button for this mental mayhem. It's like switching off the TV when you've had enough of a never-ending soap opera. Instead of getting caught in the whirlpool of rumination, you embrace mental clarity.

But it's not just about taming your inner chatter; mindfulness toughens you up. It's your boot camp for resilience. When life throws curveballs your way, mindfulness stands by your side, whispering, "You've got this." It's like a mental shield, helping you bounce back from adversity with newfound strength.

Now, let's venture into the realm of physical health. Mindfulness is more than a mental exercise; it's a healer. Imagine you're plagued by chronic pain, the relentless throb of a constant companion. Mindfulness steps in like a skilled conductor, changing the melody of pain. It's a powerful tool for pain management, making discomfort more bearable.

But that's not all – mindfulness extends its caring hand to your heart, quite literally. It lowers blood pressure and promotes cardiovascular health. It's like a personal trainer for your heart, ensuring it stays in top-notch condition.

And for those restless nights when sleep evades you, mindfulness is your lullaby. It ushers in relaxation and peaceful slumber. It's like a bedtime story for your mind, gently guiding you into the realm of dreams.

But perhaps the most magical aspect of mindfulness is its ability to bridge the gap between mind and body. It's like a handshake between your thoughts and your physical being. Through mindfulness, you become more attuned to your body's needs, making healthier choices and improving your overall physical awareness.

As we delve into this journey towards mental and physical vitality, remember that mindfulness is your guiding light. It's the compass that points you towards a balanced and harmonious life. It's a practice that invites you to embrace the present moment and weaves a tapestry of well-being that encompasses both mind and body.

So, my fellow explorer of the inner and outer realms, fasten your seatbelt and prepare to be amazed. Mindfulness is not just a trend; it's a timeless art, a profound way of life. It's a journey, an adventure, and a transformative force that will leave no stone unturned in the pursuit of your well-being.

CHAPTER - II

Basics of Mindfulness

The Concept of Here and Now

Let's take a playful leap into the enchanting realm of mindfulness, where *"Here and Now"* is not just a catchphrase but a way of life. It's like dancing to your favorite song without a care in the world, except that this dance happens in the theater of your mind.

You see, mindfulness is all about being present, and we're not talking about being physically present while mentally vacationing on a tropical island. No, it's about being here, right now, fully engaged with whatever life throws your way.

Picture this: you're sitting in your favorite coffee shop, sipping that perfectly brewed latte. But instead of savoring every drop, you're mentally juggling your never-ending to-do list. Sound familiar? It's a scene we've all played a part in. The good news? Mindfulness is your backstage pass to life's grand show.

Jon Kabat-Zinn, the guru of mindfulness, once said, "The little things? The little moments? They aren't little." And that's precisely what mindfulness is all about — realizing that every moment, no matter how seemingly insignificant, is a treasure waiting to be discovered.

So, what's the big deal about being present, you ask? Well, imagine this: you're at a beautiful park on a sunny day, surrounded by lush greenery and the sound of chirping birds. It's a scene straight out of a nature documentary. But instead of basking in this natural wonder, your mind is replaying yesterday's argument or fretting about tomorrow's presentation. It's like going to the movies and spending the entire time in the concession stand line. You miss the main event!

Being present is your backstage pass to life's grand show. It's like upgrading from nosebleed seats to a front-row view. It's about savoring the rich tapestry of life – the taste of your favorite meal, the warmth of the sun on your skin, the laughter of a loved one – without the nagging distractions of yesterday's regrets or tomorrow's worries.

Think of mindfulness as the ultimate life-enhancing app. It's the one that helps you declutter your mental space, allowing you to fully appreciate the here and now. It's like Marie Kondo for your mind – sparking joy in every moment.

Now, let's talk about meditation – the heartbeat of mindfulness. It's not about sitting cross-legged on a mountain, seeking enlightenment (unless you're into that sort of thing). It's about focusing your attention on the present moment, like a spotlight on center stage.

Imagine you're meditating, and your mind decides it's the perfect time to rehearse your embarrassing high school moment for the millionth time. Instead of getting frustrated, mindfulness gently nudges you and says, "Let's come back to the breath, shall we?" It's like having a gentle tour guide through the labyrinth of your own thoughts.

Being present is not just about avoiding the mental time-travel; it's about embracing life's full spectrum – the joy, the sorrow, the mundane, and the extraordinary. It's about becoming the curator of your own experiences, assembling a gallery of moments that define your life's masterpiece.

Definition and Origin of Mindfulness

Welcome to the ancient art of mindfulness, where being present is not just a momentary act but a way of life. Picture this: you're standing at the edge of a serene lake, the water as still as your grandma's knitting needles. At that moment, you're not thinking about your overflowing inbox or the laundry waiting to be folded; you're simply there, fully engaged with the ripples on the water's surface.

Now, let's dive into the nitty-gritty of mindfulness. It's not just about daydreaming by the lake; it's a state of conscious awareness. Imagine your mind as a curious explorer, fully attuned to the present moment, without judgment or distraction. It's like your mental GPS, guiding you through the labyrinth of life's experiences.

Dr. Jon Kabat-Zinn, the Jedi Master of mindfulness, once defined it as "paying attention in a particular way: on purpose, in the present moment, and nonjudgmentally." It's like saying, "Hey, mind, we're going to focus on this moment, and we're leaving our judgmental glasses at home." It's like a mental superhero stance – poised, intentional, and judgment-free.

According to the *American Psychological Association (APA)*, mindfulness is "a moment-to-moment awareness of one's experience without judgment." It's not a one-off event; it's an ongoing affair with each moment life serves up. It's like being a connoisseur of life's flavors, savoring every bite without assigning a good or bad label to them.

The origins of mindfulness are akin to exploring the ancient roots of a sacred tree that has provided sustenance to humanity for countless generations. This transformative practice traces its lineage to the fertile grounds of Eastern meditation traditions, particularly within the profound teachings of Buddhism.

Picture the serene scenes of monks nestled in the heart of age-old monasteries, their beings enveloped in contemplative serenity, resembling the tranquil surface of a still pond. Within the folds of Buddhism, mindfulness meditation has been nurtured and cultivated for centuries. It serves as a cherished instrument for nurturing mental and emotional well-being, fostering spiritual evolution, and even achieving enlightenment. This practice is akin to a timeless recipe, lovingly passed down through the annals of generations, preserving its wisdom and potency throughout the ages.

In the words of the *Dalai Lama*, "The mind is like a parachute; it works best when opened." The essence of mindfulness, deeply rooted in Buddhist philosophy, aligns with this wisdom. It encourages individuals to open the parachute of their minds, allowing them to glide gracefully through the skies of inner awareness and transformation.

But Buddhism isn't the only ancient tradition to embrace mindfulness. Hinduism, another old-timer, has been practicing mindfulness through various meditation techniques for thousands of years. It's like two old friends, Buddhism and Hinduism, sharing their mindfulness secrets over tea.

In Hinduism, they've got a treasure chest of mindfulness practices, from yoga to pranayama (breathing techniques) to mantra meditation. These practices aim to tame the wild stallion of the mind, to cultivate inner stillness, and to shine a light on self-awareness. It's like having a toolkit for inner exploration.

Now, here's the kicker: these ancient practices aren't just relics of the past; they're the foundation of modern mindfulness. Think of it as the old-school vinyl records that inspired today's hit songs. The wisdom and techniques passed down through generations have shaped the mindfulness practices we now use to promote health, well-being, and self-awareness.

But hold on, there's more to this story. Modern psychologists and researchers have also jumped on the mindfulness train. They've taken these ancient practices and adapted them into evidence-based interventions for a wide range of mental and physical health conditions. It's like giving an old recipe a modern twist, making it accessible to everyone.

How to practice mindfulness

So, here's the deal: to practice mindfulness, you don't need to climb a Himalayan mountain or sit in a lotus position. You can start small, like a baby step towards a more mindful you. Find a cozy corner, preferably one without nosy squirrels or chirping birds (unless you find them soothing), and sit or lie down comfortably. This is your mission control center.

Now, let's talk about your breath. It's like the trusty sidekick in your mindfulness adventure. Close your eyes if you like (just don't doze off), and focus on your breath. Feel the rise and fall of your chest or the gentle rhythm of your breath. It's like catching a ride on the breath train, and you're the conductor.

But wait, here's where it gets interesting. Your mind, being the mischievous trickster that it is, will start throwing thoughts at you – to-do lists, dinner plans, that embarrassing moment from high school. It's like a monkey with a suitcase full of thoughts crashing your serene party. But here's the twist: don't judge those thoughts. Let them waltz in, take a twirl, and gracefully exit.

If your mind insists on wandering into the past or planning the future, don't worry. It's like a GPS recalculating your route – just gently steer it back to the present moment. Think of it as a mindful boomerang; you throw it out, and it always comes back.

But wait, there's more! Mindfulness isn't just a "sit in a corner and meditate" gig. You can sprinkle it throughout your day like confetti. Imagine doing the dishes – a chore most people dread. Instead of daydreaming about winning the lottery, focus on the sensations in your hands, the warmth of the water, the sound of the bubbles. It's like turning a mundane task into a sensory spa day.

Now, let's talk about multitasking. We've all been there, juggling work emails while cooking dinner and texting your friend about weekend plans. It's like a circus act without the applause. But with mindfulness, you can be fully present in each moment. When you're cooking, savor the aroma, feel the textures, and taste the flavors. When you're texting, immerse yourself in the conversation. It's like being a mindfulness ninja, stealthily savoring each moment.

And guess what? Mindfulness isn't a one-size-fits-all deal. There are more flavors of mindfulness than there are ice cream at a summer carnival. From mindful walking to mindful eating, the possibilities are endless. It's like having a buffet of mindfulness practices to choose from – you pick what suits your palate.

Picture yourself as an adventurous kid in a playground full of exciting things to discover. You're curious and eager to explore every nook and cranny. That's just how you should approach mindfulness. Imagine each moment as a hidden treasure waiting to be uncovered. Be open to it, like a friend with a warm heart and a playful spirit. Sometimes, add a touch of humor to keep things light. No matter if you're just starting or you've been doing mindfulness for a while, remember that everyone begins as a beginner. Even the experts were once new to this. Think of mindfulness as a beautiful journey, like going on a treasure hunt. But here, the real treasure isn't gold or jewels; it's the incredible richness of each moment you discover along the way. So, savor every moment of this adventure!

CHAPTER - III

Techniques for Focusing Your Mind

Let's embark on a mini adventure into the magical world of focusing your mind. Imagine you're trying to wrangle a bunch of energetic puppies. They're running wild, bouncing off the walls, and you're just trying to get them to sit still for a moment. Sounds like a handful, right?

Well, fear not, because we've got some tricks up our sleeves, and they're as simple as they are effective.

First up, we have deep breathing – the Jedi mind trick of mindfulness. It's like taking a mini vacation without leaving your seat. Imagine you're blowing up a balloon, slowly and steadily. As you inhale, feel your belly rise like a gentle wave, and as you exhale, let go of all that puppy-like energy. It's a breath of fresh air for your mind, helping you calm the chaos.

Now, let's talk about affirmations and mantras – the verbal magic spells of focus. It's like having your own personal cheerleader. Pick a positive phrase or word, something that resonates with you. It could be *"I am calm and focused"* or *"Peace is within me."* Repeat it like you're giving a pep talk to those rowdy puppies. Let the words sink in, like a soothing melody for your mind.

And last but not least, we have visualization – the art of painting mental pictures. It's like watching a movie in your head. Close your eyes and imagine a serene beach, the waves gently kissing the shore. Feel the warm sand beneath your toes, hear the seagulls in the distance, and let your mind wander in this tranquil landscape. It's like a mental vacation, no passport required.

So, whether you're a hands-on learner, a chatterbox of affirmations, or a daydreamer extraordinaire, there's a focus technique for you. It's like having a toolbox filled with tricks to wrangle those playful mental puppies. The best part? You don't need a trainer's license; you can do it all from the comfort of your mind.

Deep Breathing

Imagine you're in the middle of a chaotic circus, with acrobats flying through the air, clowns honking their noses, and a lion roaring in the background. Now, in the midst of this whirlwind, you're handed a simple tool – a balloon. You take a deep breath and start blowing it up, slowly and steadily. As you do, the chaos around you starts to fade, and suddenly, you're in a bubble of calmness amidst the circus madness. That, my friends, is the magic of deep breathing – the art of finding tranquility in the midst of life's crazy circus.

In our fast-paced lives, we often forget the incredible power of something as ordinary as our breath. We're so caught up in the whirlwind of tasks, responsibilities, and the never-ending circus of modern life that we rarely take a moment to just breathe. But deep breathing isn't just about oxygenating your lungs; it's a ticket to the present moment, a portal to serenity, and a tool for navigating life's challenges with grace.

Deep breathing is like a secret code to unlock a treasure chest of benefits for your mind and body. It's the key to a calm and focused mind, a relaxed body, and a profound sense of presence. It's the pause button in the middle of life's chaos, allowing you to catch your breath and find your center.

When you engage in deep breathing, you're not just inhaling and exhaling; you're activating your body's relaxation mode. Your heart rate slows down, your blood pressure eases up, and those stress hormones take a breather. It's like you're waving a magic wand that transforms the circus into a peaceful garden.

So, how does it work? It's as simple as a child blowing bubbles on a sunny day. You inhale deeply through your nose, allowing the breath to fill your lungs like a gentle breeze filling a sail. Then, you exhale slowly through your mouth, releasing all the tension and stress. It's a rhythm that dances between your body and mind, bringing harmony and balance.

The beauty of deep breathing is that it's not a once-in-a-lifetime trick; it's a skill you can practice anywhere, anytime. With each intentional breath, you're anchoring yourself in the present moment, shedding worries about the past and future. It's like having a lifeline that keeps you tethered to the here and now.

In the pages ahead, we'll take a deep dive into the world of deep breathing. We'll explore its practical applications in mindfulness, and we'll uncover its treasure trove of benefits. It's not just about calming the chaos; it's about enhancing your self-awareness, boosting your focus, and nurturing your emotional well-being.

So, as you read on, imagine that balloon in the circus. With each page, you're blowing it up, filling it with the wisdom of deep breathing. And as you do, the circus around you starts to fade, leaving you in a bubble of tranquility. Here are some tips for incorporating deep breathing into your mindfulness practice:

The Technique

Imagine you're about to embark on a thrilling roller coaster ride, but before the adrenaline rush begins, you're handed a secret weapon — a magical breathing technique. Yes, that's right, deep breathing can be your superhero cape in the rollercoaster of life.

So, let's uncover the powers of this simple yet extraordinary technique.

Step 1: Find a Comfortable Posture

First things first, you need to find your comfiest superhero pose. You can sit in a chair, feeling as stable as a superhero on solid ground. Or, for that extra flair, you can go cross-legged on a cushion, looking as zen as a meditating guru. If you're feeling particularly dramatic, you can even lie down, making sure you have all the superhero-level comfort you need.

Step 2: The Ultimate Relaxation

Now, it's time to let go of all that tension. Imagine you're shedding your everyday disguise, just like Clark Kent becoming Superman. Drop those shoulders, release the stress from your face (you're not saving the world right now), and let that jaw of yours relax. Go through your body like a detective scanning for clues, and consciously let go of any tight spots or discomfort. You're preparing for superhero-level relaxation, after all.

Step 3: Meet Your Sidekick – Your Breath

Enter your trusty sidekick – your breath. Close your eyes and let your breath take center stage. Feel it like a gentle whisper as it enters and exits your body. You can choose your favorite sensation – maybe it's the rise and fall of your mighty abdomen, the chest expansion that rivals the Hulk, or the subtle airflow through your nostrils that even Spider-Man would envy.

Step 4: The Grand Inhale

Now, it's time for the grand entrance. Take a slow, deep inhale like you're absorbing the power of the universe through your nose. Let the breath fill your lungs as if you're inflating your superhero suit. Feel your abdomen rise majestically, and notice the proud expansion of your chest. You're not just breathing; you're becoming one with the breath, a true breath superhero.

Step 5: Embrace the Pause

At the pinnacle of your inhale, take a brief pause. Hold your breath briefly and revel in the stillness. You're like a statue of mindfulness, fully present in this moment. The world can't rush you; it can't distract you. You're the master of the pause, the Zen Ninja.

Step 6: The Grand Exhale

Now, it's time for the grand exit. Exhale slowly, like you're letting out a sigh of relief after saving the day. Release the breath through your nose or mouth, and feel your abdomen contract gracefully. Your chest gently falls, like a superhero retiring after a long day of heroics.

Step 7: Pause briefly again

At the end of your exhale, pause once more. Enjoy this moment of stillness before you're off on your next heroic adventure. Let go of any lingering tension or thoughts; you're in the here and now, ready for whatever comes your way.

Repeat these breathing cycles for as long as you like. Keep your focus on the sensations of your breath – the air swirling through your nostrils, the rise and fall of your chest. If your mind starts plotting world domination or grocery lists, gently guide it back to the breath, no judgment needed.

Incorporating this deep breathing technique into your mindfulness arsenal can be your secret weapon. It can reduce stress, making you as cool as a cucumber in high-pressure situations. It enhances your focus, turning you into a concentration wizard. And, above all, it promotes relaxation and well-being, making you the superhero of your own life story.

So, there you have it – deep breathing, your trusty sidekick in this grand adventure called life. With every inhale and exhale, you're not just breathing; you're embracing the fullness of the present moment, ready to tackle whatever comes your way.

Practical Application of Deep Breathing in Mindfulness

Let's dive deeper into the magical world of deep breathing in mindfulness. Think of deep breathing as your trusty Swiss Army knife; it's versatile and ready for action in various situations.

Mindful Breathing Meditation

Imagine this: You find a quiet spot, away from the chaos of everyday life. You sit down comfortably, like a zen master ready for action. It's just you and your breath. That's right, it's time for a mindful breathing meditation.

Deep breathing takes center stage here, like the opening act of a blockbuster movie. You focus on your breath, inhaling the good vibes and exhaling the stress. It's like the red carpet of meditation techniques, rolling out for your breath's grand entrance. With each inhale and exhale, you're cultivating mindfulness, like a gardener nurturing precious flowers. Your meditation experience just got an upgrade.

Mindful Transitions

Life's a series of scenes, and we often transition from one to the next like actors in a play. But wait, you've got a secret weapon – deep breathing.

Picture this: You're about to tackle a new task or move to a different place. Instead of rushing in like a bull in a china shop, you pause. You take a few deep breaths, like a superhero gearing up for action. With each breath, you ground yourself in the present moment. It's like your own mini superhero transformation sequence, complete with dramatic music.

Stressful Situations

We all have those moments when stress and challenging emotions come crashing down like a ton of bricks. But guess what? Deep breathing can be your superhero cape.

Imagine you're faced with a stressful situation. Before you dive into panic mode, you pause. You engage in deep breathing, as if you're activating your calm mode. Your stress response is tamed, like a wild beast turning into a cuddly kitten. You gain a moment of calm and clarity, ready to tackle the situation with wisdom and grace.

Daily Check-Ins

Life's a wild ride, and sometimes we forget to check in with ourselves. But deep breathing offers you a daily pit stop for self-reflection.

Picture this: You take a few moments in your day to close your eyes, like a secret agent going undercover. You breathe deeply, as if you're tuning in to your own frequency. It's like a self-check-in at the airport of life. You become aware of your physical and emotional state, identifying any turbulence. With this newfound self-awareness, you make conscious choices to support your well-being. You're the pilot of your own destiny.

Think of deep breathing as your trusty companion on your mindfulness adventure. It's not just about taking in and letting out air; it's like having a loyal friend by your side as you navigate life's ups and downs. Your breath is like a passport that takes you to a place of peace, focus, and self-understanding. It's a powerful tool in your mindfulness toolbox that can help you stay calm and centered..

So, there you have it – deep breathing, the multi-purpose tool for your mindfulness journey. It's not just a technique; it's your passport to a greater sense of calm, focus, and self-awareness. Embrace the power of your breath and let it lead you on a journey of mindfulness and inner transformation.

Affirmations

Affirmations are like secret agents working for your mind. They might seem like ordinary words, but they have a superpower – the power to influence your thoughts, emotions, and how you perceive the world. Imagine them as your mind's best buddies, always there to remind you of your inner strength and positivity. They can help you stay focused on your goals and maintain a positive outlook on life. In the world of mindfulness, affirmations are like little gems that can boost your confidence and well-being. Buckle up; it's time to unleash their superpowers!

Affirmations vs. Mind-Munching Monsters

In the world of mindfulness, affirmations and mantras are like your trusty shield against mind-munching monsters. You see, these monsters are those pesky negative thoughts that creep into your head, making you doubt yourself and the world.

Now, imagine this: You're armed with an affirmation or mantra. It's like having a superhero costume hidden under your clothes. When those mind-munching monsters show up, you whip out your affirmation, and bam! You redirect your thoughts and take charge of your mind. It's like a scene from a superhero movie, but it's happening in your head!

The Power of "*I Am*"

Affirmations often start with *"I am."* These two little words pack a punch. Affirmations are like magic spells for your mind. They are short, positive statements you say to yourself to boost your confidence, mood, and outlook on life. They often begin with the words *"I am."* Imagine these affirmations as tiny but mighty superheroes. The phrase *"I am"* is like their secret code, and each affirmation is a unique superpower. When you say, *"I am strong,"* you're not just uttering words; you're activating your inner strength. It's like summoning a superhero who's incredibly powerful and ready to face any challenge. Similarly, when you declare, *"I am calm,"* you're not just saying it casually. You're invoking your calm and composed superhero. This superhero helps you stay cool and collected even in stressful situations. And when you affirm, *"I am confident,"* you're calling upon your self-assured superhero. This superhero boosts your self-esteem and helps you believe in yourself. Saying, *"I am happy,"* introduces your cheerful superhero. This hero spreads positivity and joy wherever you go. Affirming, *"I am loved,"* welcomes your beloved superhero. This hero reminds you of the love and support you have in your life. When you pronounce, *"I am successful,"* you're beckoning your achievement superhero. This hero motivates you to reach your goals and attain success. And with the affirmation, *"I am healthy,"* you bring forth your wellness superhero. This superhero encourages healthy habits and well-being. Lastly, saying, *"I am at peace,"* invites your serene superhero. This hero helps you find tranquility and balance amidst life's chaos. So, these affirmations starting with *"I am"* are like a collection of superheroes in your mind, each with their own unique abilities. When you use them, you're not just reciting words; you're calling upon these inner superheroes to empower and guide you through life's adventures. They remind you of your strengths and help you overcome challenges with confidence and positivity.

Mantras

Mantras are like your personal cheerleaders, chanting positive vibes in the background of your mind. They've been used for centuries in mindfulness practices, originating from ancient wisdom. It's like having the wisdom of the ages on speed dial. A mantra is a word, phrase, or sound that is repeated during meditation or as a way to focus and calm the mind. It's like having your own personal cheerleaders because mantras are designed to uplift and encourage you. They can be a source of inspiration and positivity in your life. "Mantras are powerful tools for transformation and self-realization." - *Deepak Chopra*. Mantras have been used for centuries in mindfulness practices. They originate from ancient wisdom and have been passed down through generations. These powerful words have stood the test of time because they have a unique ability to shape your thoughts, feelings, and perception of the world around you. "Mantras are not small things, mantras have power. They are the mind vibration in relation to the Cosmos. The science of mantra is based on the knowledge that sound is a form of energy having structure, power, and a definite, predictable effect on the chakras and the human psyche." - *Yogi Bhajan*. They've been used for centuries in mindfulness practices, originating from ancient wisdom. The use of mantras in mindfulness practices has a rich history. Many cultures and spiritual traditions have recognized the profound impact that repetitive, meaningful sounds or phrases can have on one's consciousness.

For example, in Hinduism and Buddhism, mantras are a central part of meditation and prayer. They are believed to connect individuals with higher states of consciousness and promote spiritual growth. In essence, mantras are like a bridge to deeper understanding and connection with your inner self. They offer a way to transcend the noise and distractions of everyday life and tap into a source of wisdom and peace that has been revered for centuries.

The Mindful Magic of Affirmations and Mantras

Incorporating affirmations and mantras into mindfulness isn't just about chanting random words. By incorporating mantras into your mindfulness practice, you infuse it with a sense of purpose and intention. Each repetition of the mantra is a reminder of your chosen positive affirmation or the sacred wisdom it embodies. It's about setting the stage for a mindful mindset. It's like decorating the theater before a big show.

When you use affirmations and mantras, you're sending a clear message to your mind: "This is the kind of show we're putting on today – one filled with positivity, self-compassion, and intention." It's like being the director of your own mind-theater, and you're choosing the blockbuster script.

Transformative Potential

As we dive deeper into this chapter, we'll explore how affirmations and mantras can transform your mindfulness journey. We'll uncover their origins, their purpose, and how you can wield them like a mindfulness superhero.

By incorporating affirmations and mantras into your practice, you tap into an incredible well of wisdom within yourself. You're like a treasure hunter finding precious gems buried in your mind's backyard. These gems align with your intentions and values, making your mindfulness journey all the more meaningful.

Understanding Affirmations and Mantras:

Let's embark on a journey into the world of Affirmations and Mantras – the ancient GPS for your mind. These nifty tools have been guiding folks for centuries through the labyrinth of their thoughts and emotions. Get ready to explore the power of positive thinking with a dash of ancient wisdom.

The Chanting Chorus of the Mind

Imagine this: Your mind is like a bustling marketplace filled with vendors selling thoughts. Some thoughts are like shiny trinkets you want to keep, while others are like overripe fruits you'd rather discard. Now, enter Affirmations and Mantras – your mind's chanting chorus.

These short, snappy phrases are like your mind's cheerleaders. They chant, *"You've got this!"* and *"You are awesome!"* over and over again. The more you repeat them, the louder they get, drowning out the negative thoughts.

Mantras: The Soundtrack to Enlightenment

Mantras are like the cool soundtracks in movies. They have ancient roots, often in languages like Sanskrit, and are like little magic spells for your consciousness. Each syllable carries a unique vibration, and chanting them is like tuning into a cosmic radio station.

Close your eyes and imagine that you are chanting *"Om"* (pronounced like *"Aum"*). It's not just a sound, it is an invisible portal to another realm of consciousness. It's like you have dialed into the universe's Wi-Fi, and you're downloading wisdom and peace.

Affirmations: The Positivity Pep Talk

Think of affirmations as friendly and encouraging messages that you can say to yourself. These are modern and relatable. Affirmations are designed to feel relatable and relevant to your life. They're not complicated or fancy; instead, they're like everyday language that anyone can understand.

They're like your personal motivational coach, always reminding you that you're capable, worthy, and downright amazing. Imagine having a motivational coach who is always there to remind you of your strengths and worth. Affirmations do just that. They're short, positive statements that help boost your self-esteem and confidence. When you repeat them regularly, it's like your inner coach is cheering you on, saying, *"You can do it! You're capable, worthy, and truly amazing!"*

Suppose you are having a very rough day, and your inner self chants, *"I am happy, healthy, and successful."* Suddenly, subconsciously you stand a little taller, and your frown turns upside down. It is like a burst of sunshine in your mind.

The Toolbox of Positivity

Imagine your mind as a workshop, and inside this workshop, you have a toolbox. This toolbox is filled with special tools that can help you improve the way you think and feel. They help you rewire your brain, toss out the mental junk, and replace it with positive affirmations. Now, think of your thoughts and feelings like little pieces of information stored in your brain. Sometimes, these thoughts and feelings can be negative or unhelpful, like junk that clutters up your mental workshop. Affirmations and mantras are like magical tools that can help you clean up this mental junk. When you use them, it's like taking out the mental trash and replacing it with positive and helpful thoughts.

It's like giving your mind a spring cleaning. Think of this process as giving your mind a fresh start, just like how you might clean and organize your room during springtime. You're clearing out the old and making space for new and positive thoughts and feelings. So, affirmations and mantras are like your mental cleaning tools. They help you tidy up your thoughts, get rid of negativity, and create a more positive and organized mental space. Just like how a clean and organized room can make you feel better, a clutter-free mind can make you feel happier and more at peace.

Here are some tools from the toolbox:

"I am in the moment" is a powerful statement that encourages us to pay close attention to what's happening right now. Instead of getting lost in thoughts about what might happen in the future or feeling sad about things from the past, it reminds us to be fully present in the present. It's like saying, *"I'm here, right now, and I want to experience and enjoy this moment without being distracted by other thoughts."* This affirmation helps us practice mindfulness, which is all about being aware of the current moment without being troubled by thoughts about what's next or what's already happened.

When you say, *"I am thankful and grateful,"* you're expressing your appreciation for the good things in your life. This affirmation encourages you to focus on the positive aspects, even when things are tough or stressful. It's like having a grateful heart that notices and values the good stuff, even if there are challenges around. It reminds you to see the bright side of life and appreciate what you have, which can make you feel happier and more content. So, this affirmation helps you cultivate a sense of thankfulness and positivity, even during difficult times.

When you repeat, *"I am happy, healthy, and successful,"* you're telling yourself some really positive things. You can say this when you wake up in the morning or throughout your day. It's like giving yourself a little pep talk. This affirmation helps you feel good about yourself and the future. It's important because when you think positive thoughts about yourself, it can lead to good things in your life. It's like planting seeds of positivity that can grow into a better and happier you. So, by saying this affirmation, you're boosting your confidence and your belief that good things are on the way. It's a bit like having your own personal cheerleader in your mind, rooting for you and your success.

When you say, *"Breathing in, Aum. Breathing out, Aum,"* it's like a special phrase you can use when you meditate or do breathing exercises. Imagine it's your secret code for relaxation.

Here's how it works: when you breathe in, you think or say *"Aum"* in your mind, like a gentle hum. It's a soothing sound. Then, when you breathe out, you do the same thing – *"Aum."* It's like a calming melody for your body and mind. It helps you feel peaceful and relaxed. It's a bit like a lullaby for your soul. You can also try something similar called *"the Hum - Sau"* technique. When you breathe in, think or say *"Hum"* with a nice, long *"Mmmmm"* sound. And when you breathe out, think or say *"Sau"* while trying to relax your shoulders with a long *"oooh"* and let out a sigh. These techniques are like little relaxation rituals. They can make you feel really peaceful and help your mind be quiet and calm, like a still pond. It's your way of telling your body and mind, *"Hey, it's time to relax and be at ease."*

As we delve deeper into this chapter, you'll discover how to use Affirmations and Mantras to supercharge your mindfulness journey. These tools aren't just words; they're your allies in the quest for a positive, mindful life.

With consistent practice and a sprinkle of dedication, you'll witness the magical shift within yourself towards the mindful path of positive living and self-discovery.

Using Affirmations and Mantras in Mindfulness Practice:

Imagine if your thoughts had magic powers. Well, maybe not magic, but the power to change how you feel and see the world. That's where affirmations and mantras come in. They're like your mind's secret sauce for staying present, being kind to yourself, and thinking positively. And guess what? You can use them to supercharge your mindfulness practice! Here are some practical ways to incorporate Affirmations and Mantras:

Setting Intentions:

Setting intentions in mindfulness is a bit like preparing for an adventure. Before you begin your mindfulness practice, take a moment to set an intention. It's like giving your mind a map for the journey you're about to undertake. Imagine you want to focus on gratitude during your mindfulness session. Your intention, or mantra, could be something like *I am grateful for the abundance in my life.* Alternatively, you might choose *I choose to see the blessings in every moment.* These mantras serve as gentle reminders of the treasure hunt you're about to embark on in your mindfulness practice. They guide your mind and heart in the direction you wish to explore. So, before you start, take a moment to set your intention, and let it be your compass as you navigate the beautiful landscape of mindfulness. It's like saying to yourself, *"This is what I want to discover and appreciate today."*

Focusing the Mind:

Let's face it; our minds can be like mischievous monkeys, hopping from one branch to another. But there's a wonderful tool to help you bring that wandering mind back to the present moment – it's called a mantra. Think of a mantra as a gentle and reassuring guide for your mind. Whether you're meditating in a quiet room or simply going about your day, you can repeat a soothing word like *"peace"* or *"love."* It's like telling your thoughts, "Hey, right now, this moment is something special." When you use a mantra, it's as if you're whispering to your mind, *"Come on, let's focus here."* You're gently nudging it back to the present moment, away from distractions and worries. It's a bit like having a secret word that reminds you to appreciate the beauty of each moment. So, when your thoughts are hopping around like those playful monkeys, remember your mantra. It's your quiet anchor, gently pulling your mind back to the here and now.

Affirming Self-Compassion:

We can be our harshest critics. But with affirmations, you can turn that around. Think about how sometimes you might be really tough on yourself, like a strict coach who never lets up. You may often find faults, doubts, or insecurities within you, and it can feel like you're your harshest critic. Now, picture affirmations as your kindest and most supportive friend. When you use affirmations, you're essentially saying to yourself, *"Hey, I deserve love and acceptance,"* or you could even proclaim, *"I am absolutely enough just the way I am!"* These affirmations are like little pep talks, and guess who's delivering them? You are! It's as if you're becoming your own biggest fan, cheering yourself on through life's ups and downs. You're changing the conversation in your mind from self-doubt to self-compassion. Instead of pointing out your flaws, you're emphasizing your worth and the fact that you are already enough.

Cultivating a Positive Mindset:

Imagine you're on a journey, and along the way, you encounter unexpected obstacles. These challenges can sometimes make you feel like you're in a tight spot, surrounded by uncertainty and difficulty. But here's where affirmations come into play. Affirmations are like your trusty map and compass, helping you navigate through life's twists and turns. They're simple yet potent phrases that act as your guiding star when things get tough. Picture them as a pair of positivity glasses that you can put on at any time. For example, when you're faced with a difficult situation, you can repeat affirmations like *"I approach challenges with resilience and optimism"* or *"I attract abundance into my life."* These words become your allies, reminding you of your inner strength and your ability to overcome obstacles. It's as if these affirmations cast a warm and encouraging light on your path, making everything seem a bit brighter and more manageable. They don't magically make problems disappear, but they do empower you with a positive mindset, which can make a world of difference in how you perceive and tackle life's challenges.

Practicing Gratitude:

Practicing gratitude is like collecting little pockets of happiness in your day. You can do this by using a gratitude mantra or affirmation, which are like magic words that help you focus on the positive. Imagine saying to yourself, *"I am grateful for the simple joys in life"* or *"I appreciate the beauty around me."* These phrases are like little bottles where you store your happy moments. When you use them, it's like opening one of those bottles and letting the warm, fuzzy feeling of gratitude spread throughout your day. So, if you ever want to carry a bit of happiness with you, just remember your gratitude mantra. It's your secret tool for finding joy in the everyday moments of life.

Think of affirmations and mantras like planting seeds in the garden of your mind. Whether you borrow some wise words from tradition or make up your own, the secret recipe is simple: repeat and believe. The more you say these positive phrases and truly believe in them, the more they become a part of you. It's like practicing a musical instrument. At first, it might sound a bit off-key, but with practice, you'll play beautiful tunes. Consistency is your trusty sidekick here. Keep repeating these affirmations and mantras, and they'll soon become your companions on your journey to mindfulness. They're like a GPS guiding you to greater awareness of the present moment, understanding yourself better, and finding inner peace. Remember, the magic happens when these words truly mean something to you. It's like your favorite song; you sing it with all your heart. So, pick the phrases that tug at your heartstrings, and say them with purpose and focus. Over time, they'll become your soundtrack, adding harmony to your beautiful life.

Visualization

In the realm of mindfulness, there's a secret tool that often gets overlooked – it's called visualization. Imagine it as a magical adventure for your mind. With this technique, you can take your mindfulness journey to a whole new level.

So, what's the deal with visualization? Well, it taps into the superpower of your mind's eye. Think of it like a mental movie that can whisk you away to places of deep understanding, relaxation, and self-discovery.

But hold on, you might be wondering, "Can thinking of rainbows and unicorns really help with mindfulness?" Absolutely! Visualization adds a dash of creativity to your practice and can make a world of difference.

This chapter is your ticket to the world of visualization within mindfulness. We'll uncover where it comes from, why it's fantastic, and how you can use it in your daily mindfulness adventures. It's time to let your imagination run wild – who knows what mindfulness wonders you might discover!

The Essence of Visualization

Visualization is like an artist's canvas for your mind. It's where you get to paint vivid mental images that burst with colors, sounds, and sensations. These mental pictures bring a touch of magic to your thoughts and feelings, creating a special connection between what you're consciously thinking and what's brewing beneath the surface.

Think of it this way: when you use your mind's eye for visualization, you're throwing a cool party where your conscious thoughts and your subconscious mind finally get to hang out and collaborate. It's like getting your inner gang together to boost your self-awareness, show yourself some self-love, and connect with the present moment. Visualization in mindfulness is like taking a thrilling dive into your own imagination, but with a purpose. It's all about getting immersed in this wonderful world you create in your head. So, get ready to explore your mind's landscapes with intention and see the magic unfold!

Understanding the Benefits:

You know what's super cool? When you put visualization and mindfulness together, it's like blending your favorite ice cream flavors – the result is even better than you imagined!

Let's dive into these awesome benefits that come with mixing up mindfulness and visualization:

Deepened Presence: Imagine you're at a magic show, and the magician has your full attention. You're not thinking about what you had for breakfast or what you'll do tomorrow. You're completely in the moment, right there in the audience. Visualization provides an anchor for your attention. Now, think of visualization as your magic trick. When you imagine things in your mind, it's like watching a fascinating show. This "show" grabs your attention and keeps it from wandering away. It makes it easier to immerse yourself in the present moment. Instead of being lost in thoughts about the past or the future, you're right here, right now. You're like a detective, exploring every detail of the moment. Think of vivid imagery like a spotlight in a dark room. It points your attention to something important. In this case, it helps you pay attention to what's happening in your mind. It enables you to explore the depths of your consciousness with clarity. Imagine you're in a clear, glass-bottom boat, floating on a crystal-clear lake. You can see all the fish and plants below the water. Visualization does something similar – it makes your thoughts and feelings clearer and easier to understand.

Stress Buster: Imagine you have a backpack full of heavy books, and it's weighing you down. Stress can feel a lot like that heavy backpack. Engaging in guided visualizations triggers the relaxation response. Now, think of guided visualizations as a friendly guide who helps you take off that heavy backpack. When you listen to their words and imagine what they're saying, it's like they're giving you a magic key to unlock relaxation. It calms the nervous system and diminishes stress. When you're stressed, your body gets all jittery, like a shaken-up soda can. Guided visualizations are like a gentle hand that stops the shaking and lets the soda settle down. This calms your body and mind. As you imagine some beautiful places or scenes in your mind, it's like creating secret hideaways where you can go to find peace. Imagine a cozy, hidden treehouse in a forest; that's your sanctuary. It offers solace in times of tension: When you're feeling stressed or worried, you can visit these mental hideaways to relax and feel safe, just like going to your favorite, comforting place.

Heightened Sensory Awareness: This means becoming more aware of your five senses: sight, hearing, touch, taste, and smell. Visualization enhances your sensory acuity. When you do visualization, it's like giving your senses superpowers. It makes them sharper and more sensitive. As you craft detailed imagery, you engage your senses: When you imagine things in your mind, like a sunny beach or a cozy forest, your brain uses your senses to make it feel real. It's like your brain turns on your senses to "see," "hear," "feel," "taste," and "smell" what you're imagining. You don't just imagine with one sense; you imagine with all of them, you create a multisensory experience. It's like you're watching a movie in your mind where you can feel the warm sun, hear the ocean waves, and even taste the salty air. Visualization tunes you into the nuances of your surroundings and inner world. "Nuances" are like tiny details or special things you might not notice usually. So, when your senses are super sharp, you can notice all the little, interesting things around you and inside you.

Emotional Regulation: This is about managing your feelings, like when you're sad, angry, or happy. Guided visualizations can facilitate emotional processing. When you do visualizations, it helps you deal with your emotions better. It's like having a map to navigate your feelings. Immerse yourself in your inner imagery. This means when you picture things in your mind, like a calm beach or a cozy room, it's like you're diving into that picture with your thoughts. It's like having a compass for your feelings. When you feel tricky emotions, you can use visualizations to understand and deal with them without getting lost or overwhelmed. Visualization helps to release emotional tension. Imagine emotions like balloons. Visualizations can help you let the air out of these balloons when they get too full, so you feel better.

Intention Manifestation: This means making your dreams and goals come true. It's like turning your wishes into reality. Visualization is a potent tool for manifesting intentions. Using your imagination is a powerful way to make your dreams happen. It's like having a magic wand to bring your goals closer to you. When you clearly picture what you want in your mind, it's like creating a movie in your head. You align your thoughts and emotions with the outcomes you seek, meaning your thoughts (what you think) and your emotions (how you feel) start to match up with what you want to achieve. Catalyzing the journey toward their realization gives your goals a big kickstart. It's like when a race car gets a fast start at the beginning of a race.

So, get ready to take your mind on a fun ride through the world of mindfulness and visualization – it's like a mental theme park where the benefits are the roller coasters you can't wait to ride!

Adding Visualization to Your Mindfulness Adventure

Starting your mindfulness journey with a sprinkle of visualization can be like adding a dash of excitement to your favorite recipe. Let's explore how you can do this:

Mindful Visualizations: You close your eyes and take slow, easy breaths. It's like you're about to go on a fantastic mental adventure. Now, think about building a secret oasis of calmness inside your mind. This oasis is a bit like a hidden paradise. Picture it however you like - it could be a sunny beach, a lush forest, or even a cozy cabin in the mountains. You get to choose! Now, here's where it gets really interesting. As you imagine this special place, use your imagination like a superpower. Feel the softness of the sand under your feet (even if you're not really on a beach). Hear the soothing sounds of the waves (even if you're far from the ocean). And soak up the peaceful atmosphere (no matter where you are). It's like going on a mini-vacation without packing a suitcase or buying a plane ticket. You're creating a magical world inside your head, and it's your very own escape from the everyday hustle and bustle. So, with mindful visualizations, you're not just daydreaming. You're making a beautiful, peaceful hideaway in your mind where you can relax, unwind, and find some tranquility. It's like having a secret happy place that's always with you, ready to bring a smile to your face whenever you need it.

Breath Awareness: Imagine you're sitting in a comfy spot, maybe with your legs crossed or in a cozy chair. You're getting ready to meditate, which is like giving your mind a peaceful spa day. Now, think about your breath – you know, the air that goes in and out of your nose or mouth. Usually, you might not pay much attention to it. But in this special moment, you're going to give your breath the VIP treatment. As you close your eyes and start to breathe in and out, let your imagination join the party. Imagine that each breath you take is a bit like the gentle ebb and flow of the ocean waves. Feel the calm, steady rhythm of your breath, just like the waves kissing the shore and then drifting back. Or maybe, you can picture your breath as a serene mountain breeze. It's cool and fresh as it enters your body, then warm and peaceful as you release it. Imagine this breeze filling you with tranquility and relaxation. Now, here's the cool part: By visualizing your breath this way, you're becoming best pals with the present moment. You're not worrying about what happened yesterday or what's coming tomorrow. You're right here, in this moment, with your breath.

Body Scan: Suppose you're lying down, all comfy and relaxed. It's like you're getting a special massage, but without anyone touching you. You're about to do something called a body scan meditation, which is like giving your body a soothing, warm hug from the inside. Close your eyes and take a few deep breaths. Feel yourself letting go of any worries or stress. Now, let's start this peaceful adventure. Imagine a soft and gentle light, like a warm, cozy blanket of sunlight, starting at the very top of your head. This light is like pure relaxation and calmness. As you breathe in and out, this light starts to slowly move down through your body. As it travels, imagine it touching every part of you – your forehead, your neck, your shoulders, your arms, your chest, your tummy, your legs, and your toes. Wherever it goes, it's like a warm, healing hug from the inside. And here's the magical part: as this light touches each part of your body, it melts away any tension, discomfort, or stress. It's like a gentle, loving wave that washes all those worries away, leaving you feeling incredibly relaxed and full of life. By the time this warm light has traveled through your whole body, you're left with a deep sense of peace and vitality. It's as if you've had a spa day for your body and soul, without even leaving your cozy spot.

Future Self Adventure: Close your eyes and imagine you have a magical time machine. But it's not a machine you can touch; it's something special inside your mind. Now, let's use this magical power to travel into the future. Imagine yourself, maybe a few years from now, looking and feeling exactly the way you want to be. You're the best version of yourself, just like a superhero version of you! Visualize yourself achieving your dreams. Maybe you see yourself as a confident artist, a successful scientist, or a super-friendly person who makes everyone smile. Imagine what your day will be like in this future. What do you do? How do you act? What kind of amazing things have you accomplished? Now, here comes the cool part, while you're visiting your Future Self, really feel what it's like to be that fantastic you. Feel the confidence, the happiness, and the success as if it's happening right now. When you're back from this imaginary journey, guess what? You've brought a bit of that amazing future back with you! You might not be a superhero yet, but you've got a taste of what it's like to be your awesome future self. This helps you see what you can achieve and who you can become. It's like having a treasure map that shows you where to go. And step by step, you can start moving toward that future you've imagined.

It's like you are about to embark on a magical journey without even leaving your seat. It's not a trip you can book tickets for, but it's a journey that can take you to the farthest reaches of your imagination. To practice visualization, the following steps needs to be followed:

- First, you need the right setting. Find a comfy spot where you won't be disturbed. Sitting or lying down works, but make sure you're as cozy as a cat curled up by the fireplace on a winter's day.
- Now, let's get those engines started. Take a few deep breaths – in through your nose, out through your mouth. Think of it as the warm-up before the big game. You're getting your mind and body in sync, ready for the creativity workout.
- Here's where the magic begins. Close your eyes and let your mind wander. Imagine a place that feels like your happy place. It could be a sunny beach, a quiet forest, or even a cozy library. Whatever floats your boat.
- Now, let's put those mental paintbrushes to work. Dive deep into your imaginary world and think about the tiny details. What colors do you see? Is the sky a brilliant blue or a calming orange? Can you feel the soft sand beneath your toes or the cool breeze touching your skin? Listen closely – do you hear waves crashing, birds chirping, or maybe just a peaceful silence? Take a deep breath – what's that delicious scent wafting through the air? Flowers, the salty sea, or maybe a fresh forest aroma?
- Now comes the exciting part. Picture yourself taking a leisurely walk through this incredible place in your mind. As you wander, soak in the beauty of what you see, hear, and even smell. Let your imagination flow freely, like you're a tourist exploring a fascinating destination within your own mind. Every step you take reveals new wonders and delights. It's like going on an adventure without leaving your comfortable spot.

You can use this imaginative superpower in real life too! Imagine you've got a big test coming up or a challenging task at work. Picture yourself acing that test, or nailing that task like a pro. See yourself doing it confidently, as if you were the superhero of the story. Or maybe you've had a rough day, and you're carrying some heavy emotional baggage. Visualize yourself setting down that baggage, one piece at a time. See yourself walking lighter and feeling happier, like you've just dropped a backpack full of rocks.

Well, aside from the fact that you've just become a superhero artist in your mind, this can actually help in real life. Visualizing success boosts your confidence and motivation. Dropping emotional baggage lightens your emotional load, reducing stress and helping you feel better.

Remember, this isn't just a one-time gig. Practice makes perfect. The more you explore your imagination, the better you get at it. And before you know it, you'll be a mindfulness master, using your creative mind to paint a brighter, happier life.

CHAPTER - IV

Applying Mindfulness to Daily Life

Mindfulness in Relationships

Ah, relationships - they can be as delightful as a cozy cup of hot cocoa on a winter's day or as confusing as trying to find that missing sock in the laundry. But fret not, because mindfulness is here to sprinkle its magic and make your relationships smoother than a perfectly frosted cake. Relationships Can Be Tricky, Right? Let's face it, folks, relationships can be like navigating a maze blindfolded – confusing, occasionally frustrating, and you might even bump into a wall (figuratively, we hope). But guess what? Mindfulness can be your secret map. So, What Is Mindfulness, Anyway? Mindfulness is like having a superpower, but without the spandex suits. It's all about being present in the moment, understanding your own emotions, and being aware of the people around you. It's like having an emotional GPS that helps you steer clear of relationship roadblocks.

The Foundation of Mindful Relationships

Suppose you're in a heated argument with your partner about who should take out the trash (again!). The tension is rising, and you can feel your blood pressure going up. But what if there was a magical switch that could turn this argument into a peaceful discussion? Enter mindfulness, your relationship GPS. Mindfulness helps us to be responsive rather than being reactive to something. Mindful relationships are like having a superpower that lets you go from being a reactive volcano to a cool and collected person.

Mindfulness can play a powerful role in enhancing relationships, whether it is with a romantic partner, family member, friend, or colleague. Here are some ways that mindfulness can improve relationships:

Self-Awareness: So, self-awareness is like looking in a mirror, but instead of seeing your face, you see your feelings and thoughts. You get to know what makes you tick, like why you get grumpy when you're hungry or why you feel anxious before a big test. Mindful self-reflection enables you to understand your triggers, emotional patterns, and communication style. If we talk about the emotional patterns, imagine you're a detective, and your mission is to solve the mystery of your emotions. Mindful self-reflection helps you spot patterns. You might realize, "Hey, I often feel stressed when I have a lot of work to do." Knowing this, you can come up with a plan to deal with stress, like taking short breaks or doing some deep breathing. Now if we talk about communication style, let me ask you, did you ever have a conversation go south real fast? Might be a lot of times. Knowing your communication style is like having a secret code. You'll understand how you talk to others and how they talk to you. Are you more of a listener or a talker? Do you prefer direct or gentle communication? When you know your style, you can navigate conversations better. It is very crucial to understand how to respond and not react. Suppose someone pushes your buttons. Without self-awareness, you might react like a firecracker, exploding with anger or frustration. But with self-awareness, you can pause, take a deep breath, and think before you respond. It's like having a remote control for your reactions. Self-awareness is like having an instruction manual for yourself. It helps you understand your quirks, strengths, and areas where you can grow. When you know yourself inside and out, you're the boss of your reactions, making tough situations easier to handle.

Emotional Regulation: Emotions are like waves in the ocean. Sometimes they're gentle, and sometimes they're huge. Mindfulness helps you ride these emotion-waves without falling off your surfboard. When your emotions are on a wild ride, it's like being in a fast car. Mindfulness tells you to pull over for a moment. Just stop, take a deep breath, and let the dust settle. This pause gives you time to think. The cool thing is, when you pause, there's no judgment allowed. It's like watching a movie without deciding if it's good or bad. You're just observing your feelings, whether they're happy, sad, angry, or somewhere in between. Before mindfulness, you might've reacted to strong emotions like a bull seeing red. But now, you're like a ninja. You don't react; you respond. You think, "What's the best way to deal with this?" It's like choosing a ninja move instead of charging like a bull. Instead of yelling, you might say, "I'm upset right now, and I need a break." Or if you're super happy, you'll share that joy with others. Mindfulness helps you turn emotional chaos into calm and constructive responses. Being an emotional person means you can handle any emotion that comes your way. You're like a Jedi master of feelings. With mindfulness, you don't let emotions push you around. You're in control, and that's pretty cool, right?

Empathetic Listening: Mindful listening means being super-attentive while the other person is speaking. It is an act of presence. You focus completely on what your friend is saying, just like they're the most important person in the world at that moment. You know those pesky distractions, like your phone buzzing or your thoughts wandering off? Well, with mindful listening, you kick those distractions out of the room. Your friend gets your full attention, and those distractions can wait. But here's where it gets even cooler. Mindful listening isn't just about hearing the words; it's like having a special listening radar. You pick up on the emotions and intentions behind the words, like tuning into a hidden radio station. So, you're not just hearing; you're really understanding how your friend feels and what they mean. When you practice mindful listening, you're showing your friend that you truly care. You're creating a space where they can share their thoughts and feelings without judgment. It's like giving them a cozy emotional blanket. And guess what? When you're a mindful listening superstar, your relationships get stronger. People feel heard and understood when they're around you, and that's like a magical bond that connects hearts.

Having Empathy: Imagine your friend is feeling really sad because they lost something that meant a lot to them. With mindfulness, it's like you can step into their shoes and understand how they're feeling. You see the situation from their perspective and think, "I totally get it, my friend. Losing something you love is tough." Mindfulness helps you connect with what others are experiencing emotionally. So, when your friend is super happy, you can feel that happiness too. And when they're sad, you can empathize with their sadness. Empathy is like having a special way to connect with others in your relationships. When you show someone that you understand their feelings, it's like giving their heart a warm and comforting hug. It lets them know that they're not alone in how they feel, and that's a wonderful thing for building strong relationships.

Mindfulness in Intimate Relationships

Ah, love - the wonderful world of intimate relationships. It's like trying to solve a Rubik's Cube made of emotions, right? Well, mindfulness is here to help you unscramble those colorful feelings. It's like you and your partner are navigating through the intricate maze of emotions, trying to communicate, and being vulnerable together. Mindfulness isn't just for solo soul-searching; it's like a relationship superpower. It helps couples connect on a deeper level. With mindfulness, you're not just living together; you're "mindfully" together. So, what's in this magical relationship toolbox? It's all about being aware of each other's feelings, thoughts, and needs. Imagine your partner's emotions as precious treasures. You're the treasure hunter, and mindfulness is your map. Mindfulness in relationships is like making your partner feel seen, heard, and valued. It's the secret sauce for connection. Imagine having a conversation where you're really there, not just physically, but with your whole heart and mind. Remember those times when a small argument turned into a big explosion? Mindfulness whispers, "No more!" It teaches you to respond, not react. It's like having a pause button before things get messy.

Practical Strategies for Infusing Mindfulness in Intimate Relationships

- **Presence in Quality Time**: It is like a magic spell for your relationship. It's like you and your partner are spending time together, but not just any time — it's the special, heartwarming kind. You both put away all those distractions, like phones or TV, and dive headfirst into the moment. It could be a lovely dinner, a peaceful walk, or a deep and heartfelt chat. You're not just physically there; your mind is right there with your partner too, like a superhero with a super focus power. It's like you're saying, "Hey world, we're in our own little bubble of love right now!"

- **Compassionate Communication**: It is like having a secret code for talking to your partner. It's a way of talking and listening that's super kind and understanding. When you talk, you use "I" statements. Instead of saying, "You make me mad when you're late," you say, "I feel upset when you're late." See the difference? It's about sharing your feelings without blaming. And when your partner talks, you listen with your heart wide open. You make them feel safe to share their thoughts and feelings. It's like saying, "Hey, I'm here for you, and I really care about what you have to say."

- **Conflict Resolution**: When you and your partner have a disagreement, you're upset, and they're upset too. Instead of arguing and making things worse, mindfulness says, "Hey, let's take a breather." So, you both step back, take a few deep breaths, and calm down. You start by recognizing your own feelings and thoughts, like saying, "I'm feeling frustrated because..." Then, you try to understand how your partner might be feeling and thinking too. It's like hitting the pause button on a heated argument, so you can both talk it out calmly and with empathy. Remember, it's not about winning; it's about finding a solution that works for both of you.

- **Respond Instead of Reacting**: When you're in a situation where someone said something hurtful, and your first instinct is to snap back in anger or get defensive. That's reacting impulsively. Now, let's bring mindfulness into the picture. Instead of snapping back, you take a moment. You step back mentally, take some deep breaths, and give yourself a second to think. During this pause, you're not reacting based on your initial emotions. You're responding thoughtfully and compassionately. You might say something like,

"I understand you have a different perspective, and I'd like to talk about it calmly." Mindfulness lets you stay cool and collected in tough situations. It helps you respond wisely, not just react in the heat of the moment.

Infusing mindfulness into intimate relationships is a transformative journey that nurtures deep connection and harmony. By embodying mindfulness principles such as presence, effective communication, and emotional regulation, couples can navigate challenges with grace and cultivate an atmosphere of understanding and empathy. Mindful intimacy is a shared path of growth, where partners not only enhance their relationship but also embark on a journey of self-awareness and self-discovery.

Transformative Journey: Just like planting seeds in a garden, you're deliberately sowing the intention to be more aware, compassionate, and present with your partner. Like seeds that need nurturing to grow into healthy plants, mindfulness in your relationship requires your care and attention. You both invest time and energy in this process, much like gardeners tending to their plants. These mindfulness "seeds" begin to sprout and grow, they bring about changes within yourselves and in your relationship. It's akin to witnessing the transformation of a seed into a flourishing tree. You become more conscious of your emotions, reactions, and how you relate to each other, leading to positive changes. Think of this journey as an exciting adventure, similar to exploring new places together. As you practice mindfulness, you discover new aspects of yourselves and your partner. You start noticing the beauty in simple moments, and your connection becomes more vibrant..

Deep Connection and Harmony: When we talk about deep connection and harmony in a relationship through mindfulness, it's like orchestrating a symphony. Imagine you and your partner as two unique instruments in this orchestra. Each of you has your own melodies, rhythms, and harmonies to contribute. Now, mindfulness acts as the conductor in this scenario. It involves being fully present with your partner, just like a conductor attentively guiding each musician. You take the time to understand their musical inclinations, to listen to them without judgment, and to appreciate their individual tunes. As you both practice mindfulness, you become more aware of your own musical notes, rhythms, and variations. This self-awareness is like understanding your own instrument's nuances—how it resonates, when it needs tuning, and the care it requires to perform at its best. With this awareness and acceptance of yourself, you can then extend the same understanding to your partner. You start noticing their melodies, rhythms, and variations more keenly. It's like recognizing the unique qualities of their instrument and how to compliment them. This deepens your connection. You learn to communicate more openly and empathetically, harmonizing your melodies with compassion. Like well-practiced musicians in an orchestra, your interactions become harmonious, and you create beautiful music together.

Mindfulness Principles: Imagine your relationship as a sailing voyage on the open sea. "Presence" is like the wind that fills your sails and propels you forward. When you're fully present with your partner, it means you're giving them your complete attention, just as a sailor needs to stay focused on the course. It's like stowing away distractions and ensuring that they have your undivided focus. Just as a ship needs care and maintenance, your relationship flourishes when you're truly there for each other. Think of "effective communication" as the navigational charts and tools for your voyage. These tools require expertise to navigate the waters successfully. Effective communication means speaking kindly to your partner and listening attentively when they speak, much like using precise navigation to reach your destination. When you communicate effectively, your relationship sails smoothly, much like a well-charted course on calm waters. Emotions are like the changing weather during your voyage – they can be unpredictable. "Emotional regulation" is your ability to navigate through these emotional tides calmly and sensibly. It's like being an experienced captain who knows how to steer through rough seas. When you manage your feelings in a healthy way, you prevent unnecessary turbulence during your journey. It ensures that your voyage remains steady and resilient even in challenging conditions.

Gracefully Navigating Challenges: Imagine your relationship as a well-crafted puzzle, with each piece representing a unique aspect of your connection. However, like any intricate puzzle, there are moments when some pieces don't seem to fit together perfectly, causing minor disruptions. These challenges in your relationship can be likened to the occasional misalignment of puzzle pieces – they may not align smoothly, but they are essential parts of the overall picture. Mindfulness serves as a specialized tool for adjusting those pieces gracefully. Instead of reacting impulsively to these challenges, mindfulness encourages you to take a step back, much like an astute puzzle solver would when encountering a misfitting piece. Just as a puzzle enthusiast might pause to consider the bigger picture and explore alternative placements, mindfulness invites you to do the same. It's like taking a moment to clear your mental space, allowing for a fresh perspective. With mindfulness, you address relationship challenges with patience and empathy, akin to how a puzzle enthusiast handles misaligned pieces with care. Instead of forcefully fitting them together, you approach the situation gently, seeking to understand the underlying causes. In essence, mindfulness helps you adjust the "puzzle pieces" of your relationship with understanding and kindness, much like a skilled puzzle solver ensures that every piece finds its place harmoniously. By doing so, you can maintain the completeness and harmony of your relationship, even when faced with challenges.

Understanding and Empathy: Visualize your relationship as a delicious recipe, where each ingredient represents a unique aspect of your connection. To cook up this flavorful dish, much like skilled chefs, both you and your partner need to understand and appreciate each other's contributions. Mindfulness serves as a special tool in this culinary journey. It helps you become more empathetic, adding depth and complexity to your recipe of understanding and compassion. This empathy is like the careful blending of ingredients, combining different flavors to create a harmonious and delectable dish. Consider empathy as the secret spice that enhances your recipe. It's the element that allows you to savor your partner's emotions and experiences fully. This shared understanding ensures that both of you co-create a culinary masterpiece of connection and harmony, much like skilled chefs crafting a mouthwatering delicacy.

Shared Path of Growth: You and your partner are like two stars in the same constellation. Each of you shines brightly with your unique qualities, aspirations, and potential. In this cosmic dance, your individual growth and collective synergy are akin to stars influencing each other's brilliance. Much like stars in a constellation, you both illuminate each other's paths, helping one another reach your fullest potential. Your relationship acts as the cosmic space that fosters mutual support and growth, just as the vast universe allows stars to shine and evolve.

Tapestry of Love: In this tapestry, the threads represent important qualities. One thread is authenticity, which means being true to yourselves and not pretending to be someone you're not. Another thread is compassion, symbolizing how you care for each other. Compassion means having a kind and understanding heart toward your partner. Another thread is compassion, symbolizing how you care for each other. Compassion means having a kind and understanding heart toward your partner. There's also a thread of mutual commitment, like a promise to be there for each other through thick and thin. It's a commitment to support and love each other. All these threads are woven together with love, the strong and beautiful foundation of your tapestry. As you both add threads to this tapestry, you do it with joy, cherishing each moment you spend together. So, your relationship, when embraced with mindfulness, is like a gorgeous tapestry made of threads of authenticity, compassion, and mutual commitment, all woven together with love and the delight of living in the present moments you share.

So, when you practice mindfulness in your relationship, you're like skilled gardeners tending to a garden of love, making it grow and thrive in the warm sunlight of the present moment.

Mindfulness in Parental Relationships

Parenting is a profound journey that presents both joys and challenges. Mindful parenting, an approach deeply rooted in mindfulness principles, offers a transformative way to navigate the complexities of raising children. Mindful parenting is like having a super tool kit. It helps you handle the ups and downs of parenting gracefully. You become more aware, more present, and more kind. It's like adding magic to your parenting skills. Mindful parenting helps you connect deeply with your children. You understand them better, and they feel closer to you. Imagine if you could help your kids have strong emotional muscles. Mindful parenting is like the gym for their emotions. It teaches them to handle feelings like sadness, anger, and happiness. You become their emotional coach. You and your kids learn and grow together, and it's a fantastic journey.

Parenting with mindfulness entails being present with your children, observing their needs and emotions, and responding with patience and compassion. Engage in activities together without distractions.

Principles of Mindful Parenting

- **Presence**: You're spending time with your child, but your mind is somewhere else. Maybe you're thinking about what to make for dinner or an email you need to send. It happens to all parents, right? Mindful parenting encourages you to be present with your children physically and emotionally. Being present means when you're with your child, you're really there with them. It's like you have special glasses that help you see, hear, and feel everything your child is experiencing. No distractions! When you're present, you can connect with your child on a deeper level. They feel like they're the most important person in the world. It's like giving them a big warm hug with your attention. Those worries about dinner and emails? Well, they can wait. When you're present, you're not letting those thoughts steal your time with your child. You're making memories together. Being present helps you notice the little things. Maybe it's a funny expression on your child's face or a fascinating bug in the park. These small moments become big treasures in your parenting adventure. Your child can sense when you're truly there.

They feel your love and care. It's like a secret language between you and your little one.

- **Creating Rituals**: Establishing mindful family rituals is like creating special traditions that go beyond the occasional celebration; they become regular day-to-day activities woven into the fabric of your family life. These rituals are not just about the occasional magic of special moments but also about the everyday magic of routine and structure. Children tend to thrive in a structured schedule because it makes them comfortable with routines, familiarizes them with the outcomes, and provides stability for their growth. Think of these rituals as your family's secret codes, guiding everyone through the journey of life together. It's like having your own set of rules that make your family bonds super strong. Imagine everyone sitting around the table, talking about their day, as part of a regular dinner ritual. This consistent practice of sharing not only food but also stories and laughter strengthens your family bonds. Bedtime rituals, such as reading a bedtime story or having a cozy chat before sleep, act like the closing chapter of a good story, a reassuring hug through words. These rituals provide a sense of security and love within your family. Knowing what to expect, like having movie night every Friday, wraps your hearts in the warmth of predictability. The beauty of these rituals is that you're not just creating special moments but also lasting memories that will bring a smile to your face when you reminisce about them in the future.
- **Non-Judgmental Acceptance**: Approach your children with an open heart, free from judgment or preconceived notions. Imagine your parents say "I'm here for you, no matter what.", instead of "You're wrong," or "You shouldn't feel like that"., That means they don't judge you; they understand you. That's what non-judgmental means. It's like having a secret hideout where you can be yourself. When your parents accept you without judging, it's like getting a big warm hug from the inside. Kids have lots of feelings and thoughts, even the messy ones. When parents don't judge, you can talk about everything, from the happiest moments to the toughest

ones. When parents accept you just as you are, it's like they're saying, "I trust you." That's like getting a golden star for being yourself. Non-judgmental acceptance is like planting seeds of love. As you grow, your relationship with your parents grows too, and it gets stronger every day.

- **Emotional Regulation**: Practice emotional regulation yourself. Sometimes, emotions can feel like a big storm inside you. Maybe you're super angry, or maybe you're really upset. That's when your superpower comes to the rescue. You take a deep breath, like a superhero getting ready for action. It's like inhaling calmness and exhaling the storm. Now, instead of reacting right away, you take a moment to think. "What's the best way to handle this?" you ask yourself. You decide how to respond. It's not about being fast; it's about being smart. Maybe you talk about your feelings, or maybe you take a break to cool down. Your superpower helps you stay calm and cool, even when things get tricky. It's like having a shield that protects you from getting overwhelmed by big emotions. And this isn't just for you, you can use it to help your family and friends when they need it too.

- **Gratitude Practice**: Every day, you and your family members take a moment to think about what you're thankful for. It could be something big, like a fun adventure, or something small, like a warm hug. Then, you gather together and share your thankful thoughts. Everyone takes turns talking about what made them smile and feel grateful that day. As each person shares, everyone else listens with love and attention. It's like giving each other little heart-shaped presents. This practice makes everyone's hearts feel lighter and happier. It's like watering a garden of positivity in your home. Not only do you feel grateful for things, but you also say thank you to each other more often. It's like magic words that make everyone feel appreciated. Over time, your family bonds become stronger. You realize that even on tough days, there's always something to be thankful for, and you have each other's backs.

Practical Strategies for Mindful Parenting

- **Mindful Moments**: Integrate mindfulness into everyday routines. When you read a book with your kids, it's not just any story; it's a "Mindful Moment." You immerse yourself in the tale, sharing giggles and questions, making it an adventure together. Preparing a meal is no longer a chore; it's a "Mindful Moment." You and your children savor each step, from chopping veggies to mixing batter, enjoying the delicious journey as much as the destination. Going for a walk is not just exercise; it's a "Mindful Moment." You all notice the colors of the leaves, the songs of the birds, and the feeling of the sun on your skin. It's like a nature treasure hunt. Even conversations turn into "Mindful Moments." When you talk, you truly listen. You put away screens and distractions, giving each other the gift of undivided attention. Simple acts like giving hugs or cuddles become even more special. You feel the warmth, the love, and the connection like never before. In these "Mindful Moments," time slows down. You realize that being together is the best gift, and you make the most of it.

- **Breath Awareness**: When you notice things are getting tricky, pause for a moment. Take a few slow, deep breaths. Picture it like filling up a balloon, then gently letting the air out. Those breaths are like a magic pause button. They give you time to collect your thoughts, even when you're tempted to react right away. When you use your superpower, you stay cool and calm. You don't jump into the storm of emotions. Instead, you show your child what it's like to handle things with patience and understanding. You're not just using your superpower for yourself; you're also teaching your child about it. They see that when things get tough, taking a breath can help us think clearly and act kindly.

- **Empathetic Listening**: When your child starts talking, focus all your attention on them. No distractions, no phone, no TV. It's all about them at that moment. Sometimes, being super means being super quiet. Let your child speak without interruption. Even if you want to jump in with advice or stories, hold back. This gives them space to express themselves. Repeat back what your child is saying. This shows that you really, truly understand. It's like holding up a mirror to their feelings so they can see that you get it. Let your child know that it's okay to feel the way they do. Whether it's excitement, frustration, or sadness, every feeling is valid in your "No Judgement Zone." Sometimes, a big, warm hug is all it takes. It says, "I'm here for you, no matter what."

- **Quality Time**: It's about spending quality time with your children. This means setting aside moments when you can truly connect with them. Find out what your kids love to do and join them in their world. Whether it's building a fort, playing with action figures, or drawing pictures, be a part of their favorite activities. Create special "time capsules" where you do something unique together. Maybe it's a weekly movie night with their choice of film, or a monthly trip to the ice cream parlor. These traditions become treasured memories. Turn off those screens! Spend time without smartphones, tablets, or TV. This helps everyone focus on each other and the fun you're having. Explore the great outdoors. Go for a hike, have a picnic in the park, or simply stroll through your neighborhood. Nature provides a fantastic backdrop for quality time. Encourage your kids to share their thoughts and feelings with you. Ask open-ended questions, and really listen to what they have to say. These conversations can lead to deeper connections. Remember, quality time isn't about quantity. It's about making the time you have count.

- **Mindful Discipline**: When addressing misbehavior, approach discipline with a calm and composed demeanor. When your child misbehaves, instead of getting angry or upset, take a deep breath. This gives you time to think clearly. Instead of jumping straight to punishment, have a chat with your little one. Ask them why they did what they did. Understanding their reasons can be enlightening. Instead of grounding or time-outs, focus on consequences. Explain that actions have results. For example, if they break a toy, they won't have it to play with. This way, they learn while still feeling loved. Every misstep can be a teaching moment. Talk to them about how to do things differently next time. This helps them grow and make better choices in the future. Consistency is key. Be sure to follow through with consequences and lessons. This shows your child that you mean what you say.

Mindful parenting is like a secret code for creating super-strong connections with your kids. It's about being present, accepting them just as they are, and handling emotions like a pro. With mindful parenting, you're building a trust bridge between you and your little ones. They know you're there for them, no matter what. Imagine teaching your kids to handle stress, anger, and other big feelings with calmness and kindness. That's the superpower of emotional regulation. Your kids feel safe to be themselves, no matter how wacky or wild. Mindful parenting isn't just for kids. It's a journey of growth for parents too. You learn as you go, and you grow together. So, embrace the adventure of mindful parenting. It's like a treasure hunt filled with love, understanding, and a few surprises along the way!

Mindfulness in Social Relationships

Social relationships form the fabric of our lives, encompassing interactions with friends, colleagues, acquaintances, and the broader community. Mindfulness, with its capacity to cultivate empathy, presence, and open-mindedness, has the power to enrich and harmonize these relationships. Life is like an enormous ocean, and the people you know are like the different ships sailing in it. Mindfulness is like the wind that fills your sails and helps you steer these relationships in the right direction. When you practice mindfulness, you're essentially equipping yourself with tools. Empathy is one of these tools, and it's like having a magical compass that helps you understand what others are feeling. Being present and open-minded are also in your toolbox. With these mindfulness tools, you can create connections that feel real and honest. It's like discovering a treasure chest of friendship where every gem represents a genuine bond. Mindfulness acts as a bridge that connects you with others. It makes understanding and empathy grow, just like strong and sturdy bridges that link one place to another. In this chapter, you'll delve into the art of using mindfulness in your social life. It's like becoming an artist who paints beautiful pictures of connections, using empathy and understanding as your vibrant colors.

Practical Strategies for Integrating Mindfulness in Social Relationships

- **Presence in Conversations**: Imagine you're having a chat with a friend, and they start telling you about something important. Now, imagine you're not just hearing their words, but you're also really, really listening to what they're saying and how they feel. That's what we mean by "presence in conversations." Think of your attention like a spotlight. When you're present in a conversation, you're shining that spotlight on your friend's words and feelings. It's like saying, "I'm here with you, and I care about what you're saying." While having a video call with your friend, you close all the other tabs and apps on your computer. That's a bit like putting away distractions in a conversation. It shows that you're giving your full focus to your friend. Being present means not just hearing the words but also understanding the emotions behind them. It's like having a special radar that picks up on how your friend feels, even if they don't say it out loud. When you're truly present in a conversation, it makes your friend feel valued and heard. It's like giving them a warm, cozy hug but with your words and attention. And that can make your bond even stronger. So, the next time you chat with someone, try to be fully there, like a spotlight shining on their words and feelings. It's a beautiful gift you can give to your friends and loved ones.

- **Authenticity**: Be authentic in your interactions. When you're authentic, it's like speaking from your heart. You're not saying things because you think you should or because it's what others want to hear. You're just being you. Think of it like this: You wear a mask sometimes to hide who you really are. When you're authentic, you take off that mask. You show the real you, and that's a beautiful thing. Being authentic also means you genuinely care about the other person. You're interested in what they have to say, and you're not just pretending to listen. It's like saying, "Your thoughts and feelings matter to me." Authenticity makes your relationships stronger. When you're real with others, they feel like they can trust you. They know you're not pretending, and that creates a deep connection. So, in your interactions with friends, family, or anyone else, try to be your true, authentic self. It's like showing them the beautiful, real you, and that can lead to wonderful and meaningful conversations

- **Open-Mindedness**: Approach interactions with an open mind. When you're open-minded, you're willing to listen to what others have to say, even if it's different from what you think. It's like saying, "I'm curious about your point of view." Instead of jumping to conclusions or deciding something before you even hear it, you take your time to understand. It's like giving ideas a fair chance to be heard. Open-mindedness is also about respecting that people are different. It's okay if they see things in a way you haven't thought of before. Being open-minded helps you learn and grow. You discover new things, see the world from different angles, and build better relationships. It's like having a colorful palette of ideas and perspectives to choose from. So, in your interactions with others, try to be open-minded. It's like saying, "I'm ready to hear what you have to say, and I respect your unique way of thinking." This makes your relationships richer and more vibrant.

- **Empathetic Responses**: When you're empathetic, you can put yourself in someone else's shoes. It's like saying, "I want to know what it's like to be you right now." You pay close attention to what they say and how they say it. It's like giving them your full, undivided attention. If they're sad or happy, you "get" them. You might say something like, "I'm here for you," or "I'm so happy for you." It's like giving them a warm hug with your words. Empathy helps you connect with people. It shows them that you care about their feelings. It's like saying, "Your emotions are important to me." So, the next time someone is happy, sad, or going through something tough, try using your empathy superpower. It's like being a kind and understanding friend.

- **Respectful Boundaries**: In any good relationship, there's something very important called "respect." What Is Respect? Respect means you treat someone the way they want to be treated. It's like saying, "I care about your feelings and what you're comfortable with." Sometimes, people have rules about their personal space or what they're okay with. Respecting boundaries means you follow those rules. It's like saying, "I'll give you the space you need." When you respect someone, they feel safe and valued. It's like telling them, "You're important to me, and I'll be kind to you." Imagine if everyone respected each other like this. That would make our relationships happy and strong.

- **Cultivate Gratitude**: Gratitude is like saying, "Thank you." It's when you show you're happy for something or someone. When you say thanks, it makes your relationships better. It's like telling people, "I'm glad you're in my life." Just say thank you or let people know you appreciate them. It's like giving them a little warm hug with your words. When you're grateful, it makes everyone feel good. It's like sharing a smile that makes your connection stronger.

- **Perspective-Taking**: Perspective-taking is like trying on different glasses to see the world from someone else's view. When you understand how others feel or think, it makes your relationships stronger. It's like building bridges between your hearts and minds. Imagine what it's like to be in their situation. It's like a fun game of pretend, but it helps you connect better with others. When you see the world from their side, it's easier to be kind and make friends. It's like having a superpower for better relationships!

- **Non-Judgmental Acceptance**: Embrace diversity and differences in social relationships. Non-judgmental acceptance is like being a rainbow on a rainy day. You shine bright, no matter the weather. When you accept others just as they are, it's like opening a door to their hearts. They feel safe and loved. Be like a friendly cat who cuddles with everyone, not just those who look like you. Celebrate the colors in the human rainbow. When you let people be themselves, they bloom like beautiful flowers. And you get a garden of wonderful friends.

Applying mindfulness to relationships transforms the way we engage with others, fostering deeper connections, effective communication, and emotional well-being. By cultivating self-awareness, regulating emotions, and practicing empathetic listening, we lay the foundation for mindful relationships. Whether in intimate partnerships, family dynamics, or social interactions, mindfulness is like a secret ingredient for better relationships. It helps you understand others and yourself. First, get to know yourself. Then, listen to others like you're reading a good book—curious and without rushing to the ending. When you bring mindfulness into your relationships, it's like planting seeds of understanding and watching them grow into beautiful, strong trees of connection.

Mindfulness in the workplace

Welcome to the wild world of work, where ringing phones, endless tasks, and shifting deadlines rule the land. It's like a never-ending game of whack-a-mole. But wait, here's your secret weapon: mindfulness! Imagine if you could tackle your to-do list with the precision of a ninja, handle office drama like a diplomat, and stay calm when your inbox explodes. That's what mindfulness brings to your cubicle. No need to transform your workspace into a meditation retreat. Mindfulness at work is about staying cool and collected amidst the chaos. With mindfulness, you become the superhero of your workspace. You'll focus better, bounce back from setbacks, and understand your coworkers' quirks like a mind reader. Yes, you can even sneak in a bit of mindfulness while sipping your double-shot latte. No need for a lotus position in the break room! Mindfulness in the workplace involves cultivating a present-moment awareness that enhances focus, decision-making, and interpersonal interactions. It's about approaching tasks and interactions with a clear mind and an open heart, thereby promoting a sense of purpose, engagement, and well-being.

Practical Strategies for Applying Mindfulness in the Workplace

- **Mindful Morning Ritual**: Begin your workday with a few minutes of mindfulness. Instead of rushing in, you take a moment to breathe and center yourself before diving into tasks. Before you open that inbox, remind yourself what you want to achieve today. Visualize your goals, prioritize tasks, and sprinkle in a dash of motivation. Inhale, exhale, repeat. Deep breaths work like magic to clear the fog in your brain and get you ready to conquer the day. You're not just another hamster on the office wheel. You're the mindful master of your work domain, ready to tackle tasks with focus and a clear mind. So, the next time you're tempted to dive headfirst into work chaos, remember your Mindful Morning Ritual.

- **Focused Task Management**: Engage in tasks with full presence. Instead of juggling, you're laser-focused on one task at a time. That means no checking emails while chatting on the phone or scrolling through social media during meetings. Because it's not about doing more; it's about doing better. When you tackle one thing at a time, you dive deep into it like a pro. You're not just scratching the surface; you're excavating treasures of quality and efficiency. Your work becomes a masterpiece, not a hodgepodge of half-done tasks. You'll finish things faster and with a higher level of excellence.

- **Meeting Mindfully**: Approach meetings with a clear mind - no mental baggage from previous tasks. You're like a sponge, ready to soak up all the information. Ever heard the phrase, "two ears, one mouth"? That's active listening in a nutshell. You listen twice as much as you speak. Your attention is like a spotlight, shining on the person talking. No mental wanderings to your to-do list. Well, it's like tuning into an interesting podcast. You catch all the juicy details, understand the plot, and can ask thoughtful questions. Your input becomes valuable because you're not just waiting for your turn to talk. Meetings become productive and engaging. No more daydreaming about lunch while your colleague presents. You're in the zone, and that makes you a meeting maestro!

- **Emotional Regulation**: Think of it as your mental brakes. When you face a tough moment, you don't just dive into an emotional pool. Nope, you pause. Take a few deep breaths. It's like pressing the pause button on your feelings. Well, let's say your boss drops a surprise project on your desk. Your first reaction might be panic or frustration. But with emotional regulation, you step back. You breathe. Suddenly, you're not reacting; you're responding. You can calmly figure out your game plan. Emotions don't control you; you control them. You're the master of your emotional universe.

- **Constructive Work Habits**: It's like creating a blueprint for productivity. You don't just jump into tasks randomly; you prioritize. You set clear goals. Imagine you have a mountain of work in front of you. Instead of panicking, you use your constructive work habits. You break that mountain into manageable chunks, prioritize what's important, and tackle each piece with focus and determination. Stress melts away, and success becomes your best buddy. You're not just busy; you're effective. It's like having a secret productivity spell. You meet deadlines without the drama, and your boss might wonder if you have a time-turner. You leave work feeling accomplished, not overwhelmed. And your coworkers? They'll want to know your productivity secret.

- **Focus on One Task at a Time**: It's like having a laser beam for your brain. Multitasking seems like a good idea, but it's a sneaky trickster. It makes you think you're doing more, but really, you're doing less, and your stress levels shoot through the roof. When you focus on one thing, your brain doesn't have to switch gears all the time. It dives deep into the task, and that's when the magic happens. Stress levels drop, and your productivity soars. You're like a superhero with a calm, clear mind. So, next time you're tempted to multitask, remember the power of one. Take a deep breath, focus, and watch as your workday becomes a masterpiece of productivity and peace.

- **Take Mindful Breaks**: These aren't your regular coffee breaks; they're like mini-vacations for your brain. Did you ever listen to your thoughts? It's like eavesdropping on your brain's secrets. Observe those thoughts and feelings without being the judgey judge. Breathe in, breathe out. It's like hitting the reset button for your brain. Feel that calm wash over you. Take a stroll, even if it's just around the office. Stretch those legs, and let your mind wander like a happy puppy in a park. Mindful breaks give your brain a breather. You're like a superhero taking a power nap, and when you come back, you're ready to conquer the world. Stress melts away, creativity soars, and your workday becomes a smooth ride instead of a rollercoaster.

- **Mindful Communication**: Instead of babbling like a waterfall, speak with purpose. Imagine every word is a precious gem, and you're placing them one by one. Know why you're talking. Are you sharing an idea, asking a question, or just spreading some office gossip? Be clear in your intention. Sometimes, silence is golden. Take a pause before responding. It's like a suspenseful movie; you're building up to the big reveal. Mindful communication cuts through the office noise. Your words become laser beams of clarity, and your ears turn into super-sponges, soaking up all the insights. Colleagues who get you, less misunderstandings, and a workplace that's like a well-oiled machine.

Mindfulness in the workplace offers a holistic approach to navigating professional challenges with grace and resilience. By embracing mindfulness principles such as focus, stress reduction, and effective communication, individuals can create a work environment that promotes productivity, well-being, and positive interactions. Imagine you're in a noisy circus, but you're so focused that even the clowns can't distract you. That's what mindfulness does. It sharpens your focus, making tasks a breeze. And sometimes we feel stressed at work, right? No more! Mindfulness is like a soothing balm for your frazzled nerves. Take a breather, relax, and let stress evaporate like morning dew. You'll speak clearly, listen like a pro, and avoid those awkward "Did I just say that?" moments. The workplace becomes more than just deadlines. It's your stage for growth. Mindfulness makes you thrive by adding intention, presence, and a sprinkle of well-being. You become the calm, collected person of your office, and you're on the path to workplace enlightenment. Work isn't just work; it's a place where you grow, shine, and spread good vibes.

Mindfulness in Daily Tasks and Routines

Amidst the hustle and bustle of modern life, our daily routines often feel like a series of checkboxes to be marked off. However, mindfulness offers a radical shift in perspective—one that invites us to infuse each moment with awareness and presence, transforming the mundane into the extraordinary. By integrating mindfulness into our daily tasks and routines, we can discover a profound sense of joy, gratitude, and purpose in even the simplest actions.

Imagine your morning coffee isn't just a caffeine fix. It's a tiny joy explosion in your mouth. That's mindfulness - turning the everyday into the extraordinary. Ever felt like a robot following the same daily script? Mindfulness breaks those chains. It's like living in HD, where every moment is alive with possibility. Whether it's folding laundry or smelling a flower, mindfulness helps you find joy, beauty, and purpose in the smallest things. Life isn't just a series of boring tasks anymore. It's a grand adventure filled with beauty and surprise. Your daily life becomes a treasure hunt for joy, gratitude, and meaning. You'll start to notice beauty everywhere, even in your morning cereal.

Here are some practical ways to practice mindfulness in daily tasks and routines

- **Mindful Mornings**: Begin your day by dedicating a few minutes to positive phrases and mindful planning of the day. Instead of jumping out of bed like it's a race, take a moment. Breathe deeply, feel the coziness of your blanket, and slowly wake up your body. Think of a few positive words or phrases. Say them quietly or in your head. It's like whispering sweet encouragement to yourself. When brushing your teeth or having breakfast, do it like it's the best thing ever. Feel the brush against your teeth, taste every bite of your cereal. Instead of morning chaos, you start the day like a graceful dancer, flowing through each step with ease. Your mornings become peaceful, energizing rituals that set a positive tone for the day

- **Mindful Breathing**: One of the simplest and most effective ways to practice mindfulness is through breathing. Look for a cozy nook where you won't be disturbed. Close your eyes if you like, and start taking slow, deep breaths. Feel the air coming in through your nose and filling your chest and belly. Then, feel it going out. If your mind starts to wander (and it will – that's normal), just notice it and gently bring your focus back to your breath. It's like giving your busy brain a vacation. You get calmer, and it's easier to deal with whatever life throws your way. You can do this anywhere, anytime. So, whenever you feel a bit "AAARGH," take a few mindful breaths, and voila, instant calm!

- **Mindful Eating**: When you eat, take the time to fully savour each bite.Find a place away from noisy TVs and phones. Take a bite of your food, but don't rush it. Feel the food in your mouth. Is it crunchy, squishy, spicy, or sweet? Let your taste buds throw a taste party! Chew your food like you're chatting with a good friend – slowly and thoroughly. While you munch, make it a date with your food. No need to invite the TV or your phone. Enjoy the peace and quiet. You become a food connoisseur, and each meal is like a fancy restaurant experience. Mindful eating isn't just yummy; it can help you eat just the right amount and feel healthier.

- **Mindful Walking**: Take a break from sitting and move your body mindfully. Go for a walk-in nature or anywhere with some nature vibes. Now, this is where it gets exciting. While walking, tune in to your senses. What colors do you see around you? Is the sky as blue as a peacock's feather, or maybe it's a soft shade of orange during sunset? Listen carefully – are there birds singing, leaves rustling, or even distant chatter of people? Feel your feet hitting the ground – is it soft like a pillow or firm like a yoga mat? Keep walking, but do it with a dash of mindfulness. It's like your body's doing a graceful dance with the world. Mindful walking turns your ordinary stroll into a magical journey. You become best pals with nature and discover its beauty in every step.

- **Mindful Listening**: When you are in a conversation with someone, practice listening mindfully. Pay super close attention to your friend's words. Pretend you're a detective solving a mystery, and their words are the clues. Hold off on your thoughts and ideas for a bit. Let your friend finish what they're saying, like waiting for your turn on a swing. Dive into the conversation like it's your favorite story. This way, you'll understand your friend better and make them feel extra special.

- **Mindful Body Scan**: Take a few minutes to lie down and scan your body for any sensations or tensions. Start with your feet and slowly move your attention up your body. Notice any areas of tightness or discomfort, and try to relax those muscles. By becoming more aware of your body, you can release tension and feel more relaxed.

- **Mindful Movement**: Find a peaceful spot where you won't be bothered. Choose a movement or exercise you enjoy and do it slowly, paying close attention to how your body feels. Notice your muscles stretching and relaxing, feel your breath, and how your joints move. Be completely in the moment, forget about everything else. If you keep doing this, it can make you stronger and more flexible, calm your stress, and make you feel more connected to your body and mind.

- **Mindful Evening Reflection**: Before you go to bed, create a peaceful evening routine. Think back on your day, recognize the things you did well and the moments when you were mindful. Let go of any remaining stress or worries. This helps you end your day on a positive note and prepares you for a restful sleep.

Mindfulness in daily tasks and routines is a testament to the transformative power of presence. By infusing your actions with awareness, you invite moments of joy, gratitude, and deeper connection into your life. Remember that mindfulness is a skill that takes practice and that it is okay to struggle at times. By practicing mindfulness regularly, you can develop greater resilience and a deeper sense of inner peace and well-being, even during difficult times. This practice reveals the extraordinary within the ordinary, allowing you to navigate your days with intention and curiosity. Through mindfulness, routines cease to be repetitive obligations—they become opportunities for personal growth, self-discovery, and a profound appreciation for the intricate tapestry of life's simplest moments. As you weave mindfulness into the fabric of your daily existence, you embark on a journey of awakened living, one that unfolds with each breath, step, and heartbeat.

Mindfulness in Difficult Situations

Life can be stressful, and even though we have the ability to handle some stress and occasional intense periods, prolonged stress can have serious consequences on our physical health, well-being, and overall quality of life.

Stress is a natural response to the challenges of life, but when stress becomes chronic, and compounded with other problems and worries, the impact on our physical and mental health can be severe. The challenge lies in the fact that we often do not have a warning when stressful life events will occur. Even if we generally feel capable of managing upsets, there will come a point where we feel overwhelmed, struggling to cope with our emotions, responsibilities, and the demands of everyday life.

The stress response is triggered when the amygdala, a part of the brain, perceives a threat. In this situation, hormones like adrenaline and cortisol are released, leading to various physiological changes. These changes include increased respiration and blood flow to the extremities and brain, heightened senses, and muscle readiness for action, among other potentially life-saving adaptations. When the threat subsides, the parasympathetic nervous system takes over to slow down the stress response and return the body to a baseline state. It is important to note that the stress response can be activated not only by obvious threats but also by psychological stress, such as feeling overwhelmed, or physical discomfort like chronic pain. Regardless of the cause, both the brain and body react in a similar manner, preparing to fight, freeze, or flight.

When our body's stress response is activated in situations that are not actual threats, it can leave us in a heightened state without a necessary outlet for that energy. This ongoing state of hyper-arousal can have significant consequences for our physical and mental well-being. Over time, the release of stress hormones and the accompanying physiological reactions can take a toll on our health. This prolonged activation of the stress response can contribute to various physical and mental health issues.

When faced with challenging circumstances, it can be easy to become overwhelmed by negative emotions such as anxiety, stress, or fear. Practicing mindfulness can be especially beneficial during those difficult situations, as it can help you to stay present and focused, and manage your emotions in a healthy way.

Here are some tips for practicing mindfulness during challenging times:

- **Mastering Mindful Respiration for Inner Calm**: When life gets tough, one simple trick can really help: focusing on your breath. It's like a secret weapon to stay calm and collected. Here's how it works: When things get tricky, take a few deep breaths. Feel the air going in and out of your body. It's like giving your mind a little break. This special kind of breathing also helps you become more aware of what's going on inside you. You can start to notice when stress is trying to sneak up on you. And guess what? When you take these deep breaths, it's like telling your body to relax. It's like flipping a switch that says, "Hey, no need to stress out right now."

- **Embrace Your Emotions Mindfully**: Facing your feelings is like looking in the mirror and saying, "I see you." When you're feeling things that aren't so easy, it's okay to give them a nod and say,

"I know you're there." Imagine your emotions are like colorful balloons. Some are bright and cheerful, while others might be a bit gloomy. When you see those gloomy balloons, don't pretend they're not there. Instead, let yourself notice them and say, "Yep, that's how I'm feeling right now." It might sound simple, but it's like a secret superpower. When you accept your emotions, it's like giving them permission to be heard. You're not trying to hide them or make them go away. Instead, you're letting them float by, just like those balloons in the sky.

- **Mindful Presence**: Try to stay present in the moment, rather than getting lost in worries about the future or regrets about the past as the real magic happens in the 'here and now'. It's like the center of the universe, the place where you're living and breathing right this second. So, when you catch your mind drifting off into time travel, gently guide it back to the present. Feel your feet on the ground, the air on your skin, and the sounds around you. It's like tuning into the coolest radio station – the one that's playing the song of your life. By staying present, you'll discover that the "now" is pretty amazing, and it's the place where you have the most power to make things better.

- **Mindful Sensory Engagement**: When you engage your senses to observe, feel and experience every detail around you, it's like you're on a thrilling adventure, exploring a world you've never fully noticed before. And guess what? That world is the present moment, and it's more incredible than any movie or book.

- **Mindful Acceptance**: Acceptance is like giving a nod to obstacles, recognizing them without getting upset. It's not giving in or saying it's okay, but more like saying, "I see you, but you won't ruin my journey." When you practice acceptance, you're like a wise traveler, knowing some hurdles are part of the adventure. You keep moving forward, step by step, with a clear mind and a heart free from worries.

- **Mindful Self-Compassion**: Be kind and compassionate to yourself, especially during difficult times. Remember that it is okay to feel difficult emotions and that you are doing the best you can. You can practice self-compassion by placing one hand on your heart or on an arm, providing soothing comfort that reminds us we are safe. As we calm ourselves, we gain a sense of clarity and spaciousness in our thinking to consider our next best action.

- **Mindful Action**: Taking mindful action means not just thinking about it but actually doing something when it's needed. Figure out what you need to do to deal with the situation and then go ahead and do it with focus and determination. It's about turning your thoughts into actions to make a positive change.

- **Cultivating Mindful Gratitude**: Practicing gratitude means taking a moment to think about the good things in your life, even when things are tough. It's like finding a little bit of sunshine on a cloudy day. This can help you feel more positive and happy, even when facing difficulties.

CHAPTER - V

Advanced Mindfulness Techniques

Advanced mindfulness techniques are like special moves in a video game. When you've become really good at regular mindfulness, these techniques take you to the next level. They help you understand yourself even better and make big changes in your life. It's like unlocking hidden superpowers for your mind. But remember, it takes practice to get there, just like mastering a tough level in a game. Here are a few examples of advanced mindfulness techniques:

Insight Meditation

Insight Meditation, also called *Vipassana*, is like a treasure chest in the world of mindfulness. It's a practice that goes way back to ancient times when wise folks explored the secrets of the mind. Imagine it as a grand adventure, like a quest in a video game. In this adventure, you become a detective, but instead of solving crimes, you're investigating your own mind and the world around you. The goal isn't to catch bad guys; it's to uncover deep truths about life and yourself. With insight meditation, you sharpen your detective skills by paying super close attention to everything. You notice how things change, how they depend on each other, and how your own mind works. It's like putting together the pieces of a giant puzzle. As you become a master detective, you start seeing the world in a whole new way. You realize that everything is connected, and nothing stays the same forever. It's like finding hidden treasures of wisdom that make your life better. So, insight meditation is your ticket to this exciting adventure, where you uncover the secrets of your mind and the world, all while becoming wiser and happier. It's a journey worth taking!

The Essence of Insight Meditation

Insight meditation is like having a front-row seat to the greatest show on Earth: life itself. It's all about looking carefully, like a scientist with a microscope, at everything that's happening in your mind and the world around you. Imagine you're sitting in a park, watching people, animals, and nature. You don't judge or get attached; you just watch. In insight meditation, you do the same thing but with your thoughts, emotions, and sensations. You become a peaceful observer. As you watch, you start noticing something incredible: everything is always changing. Just like clouds drifting in the sky, your thoughts and feelings come and go. This realization is like finding a hidden treasure because it helps you understand that you don't have to be upset by things that change. It's like learning the secret of a magic trick. You see how suffering happens when we want things to stay the same, but they never do. Insight meditation helps you understand this and shows you the path to feeling free and content. So, at its heart, insight meditation is all about watching the show of life, discovering how things change, and finding the wisdom to be truly happy. It's like becoming a master of life's mysteries!

Historical Origins

Think of Vipassana meditation like an ancient treasure map passed down through generations. A long, long time ago in ancient India, a wise man named *Siddhartha Gautama* became the *Buddha,* which means *"the awakened one."* He discovered profound truths about life, suffering, and how to find peace. He shared his wisdom with his followers, and some of those teachings were written down. One of these writings is the *Satipatthana Sutta,* like a special guidebook to understand our minds and the world around us. Centuries later, in Burma (now Myanmar), a meditation master named *MahasiSayadaw* dusted off this ancient guidebook. He took the old teachings and gave them a fresh twist, making them accessible to people in his time. Then, in the 20ᵗʰ century, another wise teacher, *S.N. Goenka* took this precious knowledge and brought it to the Western world. He made it possible for people from different cultures to learn and benefit from these ancient insights. So, Vipassana meditation is like a journey through time, with teachings that started with the *Buddha*, got a makeover from *MahasiSayadaw*, and then traveled the world thanks to *S.N. Goenka*. It's like a timeless gift that keeps on giving, helping people find peace and understanding in our modern lives.

Techniques and Practice

Insight meditation involves cultivating moment-to-moment awareness of your physical sensations, mental processes, and emotional states. Here is a general overview of the practice:

- **Anchoring Awareness**: Imagine your mind is a boat, and your thoughts are waves on the water, sometimes calm and sometimes choppy. To navigate this sea of thoughts, you need an anchor—a stable point to keep you from drifting away. In insight meditation, your anchor is something simple and constant, like your breath or the gentle movement of your belly as you breathe. So, when you start your meditation, you focus all your attention on this anchor. It's like tying your boat to a strong, unmovable rock. As your thoughts come and go like waves, you stay connected to this anchor, keeping you steady and present in the moment. This anchoring helps you explore the depths of your mind with clarity and calmness.

- **Observation of Sensations**: During insight meditation, you become like a gentle scientist studying your own body. As you focus on your breath or other anchor, pay close attention to the sensations happening in your body. These sensations can be all sorts of things – warmth, coolness, tingling, or even a little tension. But here's the interesting part: Instead of reacting to these sensations or trying to change them, you become like a curious explorer. You simply watch them. It's as if you're observing the changing colors of the sky at sunset – you don't try to paint the sky; you let it change on its own. In the same way, you let these sensations in your body be as they are. You don't hold on to them or push them away. This calm observation helps you understand more about yourself and the way your body and mind work.

- **Embracing Silence or Mouna**: Within the realm of insight meditation, the practice of "Mouna," or embracing silence, occupies a profound and transformative place. It serves as a means to enrich one's awareness and strengthen the connection with the present moment. Select a tranquil and undisturbed setting where meditation can unfold without the intrusion of external noises, now shift the focus towards nurturing internal silence. Embracing silence means allowing these mental processes to naturally arise and dissolve while maintaining a stance of detachment and non-reactivity. By directing your attention to the gentle ebb and flow of your breath, you establish a stable point amidst the fluctuating currents of the mind. This serves as a gradual pathway to quieting the mental noise, allowing you to remain rooted in the present moment. It's crucial to recognize that embracing silence does not equate to suppressing thoughts or coercing the mind into a state of emptiness. Instead, it encourages non-engagement with the continuous stream of thoughts. You acknowledge the thoughts as they arise and allow them to pass without becoming entangled in their content. As you continue to engage with the practice of Mouna, you'll likely notice a gradual expansion of your awareness. By embracing silence, you create spaciousness within your consciousness for a more profound connection with your physical sensations, mental processes, and emotional states.

- **Thoughts and Emotions**: Imagine you're sitting by a river, and as you watch, leaves and twigs float downstream. During insight meditation, your thoughts and emotions are like those things floating by. They come into your mind, stay for a while, and then drift away. Instead of trying to hold onto them or push them away, you simply watch. You don't judge them as good or bad; you see them as temporary visitors. This practice helps you let go of the strong hold these thoughts and emotions might have over you. It's like realizing that, just like the river, your mind is always moving, and things will naturally come and go.

- **Cultivating Equanimity**: In insight meditation, equanimity plays a crucial role. Equanimity is like being a calm and unbiased referee in a game. In insight meditation, you watch your thoughts and feelings as they come and go, just like players on the field. Equanimity helps you not to favor any side. You don't get overly excited when something pleasant happens in your mind, and you don't get upset when something unpleasant occurs. It's as if you're watching a game without rooting for either team. This calm and balanced approach allows you to see things clearly and make wiser choices in life.

- **Deepening Insight**: Over time, as you continue practicing, you may experience moments of profound insight. Deepening insight is like peeling an onion. When you practice insight meditation over time, you start to uncover deeper truths about life, just like peeling away layer by layer of an onion. These truths are about three things: impermanence, which means everything changes; unsatisfactoriness, which means clinging to things can bring suffering, and not-self, which means there's no unchanging self in you. It's like discovering the hidden secrets of life through your own experience, and it can lead to a deeper understanding of how the world works..

Impact of Insight meditation

Insight meditation is a transformative practice that enhances various aspects of mindfulness:

- **Deeper Self-Understanding**: Deepening self-understanding is like becoming friends with yourself. When you watch your thoughts and feelings closely during insight meditation, you start to understand how your mind works. You notice what makes you happy, what upsets you, and why you react in certain ways. This understanding is like having a guidebook to your own mind and heart, and it helps you respond to life's challenges with more awareness and choice, instead of reacting automatically.

- **Enhanced Mindfulness**: Imagine your mind is like a detective searching for clues in the present moment. With insight meditation, you're giving your inner detective a magnifying glass to see even the tiniest details. It's like going from watching a movie in standard definition to suddenly experiencing it in high definition. You notice things you've never seen before—the colors, the sounds, the textures of life become vivid and clear. This heightened awareness helps you break free from old habits of thinking and reacting, allowing you to respond to life's challenges and joys with greater wisdom and clarity.

- **Embracing Impermanence**: When you practice insight meditation, you start to truly grasp that everything in life, just like the water in the river, is always moving and changing. The trees grow, the seasons shift, and even your thoughts and feelings come and go like ripples in the water. Instead of trying to hold onto things that are always changing, you learn to go with the flow. When changes come, you don't resist or panic; you adapt and find your balance. This understanding of impermanence becomes your compass, guiding you through life's ever-shifting landscapes with a sense of calm and acceptance.

Insight meditation (*Vipassana*) is a profound journey into the heart of mindfulness practice. This practice deepens self-awareness, fosters equanimity, and enhances your ability to engage with the present moment authentically. As you embark on the path of insight meditation, you open the door to a transformative experience that not only shapes your mindfulness journey but also offers a profound understanding of the nature of existence and the liberation that arises from clear seeing. Through this practice, practitioners can develop greater insight into the nature of reality and the impermanence of all things. This can lead to a greater sense of equanimity, compassion, and freedom from suffering, giving rise to greater questions of self and taking in the bigger picture.

Hence, Insight mindfulness meditation can be challenging for beginners, as it requires a high level of concentration and self-awareness and it might be too big of a bite to start off with. It is often recommended that practitioners start with shorter meditation sessions and gradually increase the duration as they become more comfortable with the practice.

Also, having a qualified teacher to guide you is really helpful. They can make sure you're on the right track and not pushing yourself too hard. With practice and the right guidance, insight meditation can be a powerful tool for gaining wisdom and insight about yourself and the world around you. It's like a lantern that lights up the path to understanding and freedom from suffering.

Metta Meditation

Metta meditation, also known as *loving-kindness meditation*, is like a warm hug for your heart. It's a practice that's been around for a very long time and doesn't belong to any specific group; it's for everyone. When you do Metta meditation, you're like a gardener, but instead of growing flowers, you're growing kindness, compassion, and love in your heart. You start by wishing good things for yourself, like happiness and peace. Then, you send these same good wishes to people you care about, like your friends and family. But it doesn't stop there; you spread these good wishes even further. You send them to people you don't know so well, like acquaintances or even people you've had disagreements with. Finally, you send these warm-hearted wishes to everyone in the world, including those you may have never met. The goal of Metta meditation is to fill your heart with kindness, compassion, and empathy, not just for yourself and your loved ones, but for all living beings. It's like watering a garden, and as you do it, you feel more connected and peaceful inside. So, Metta meditation is like a magic spell that helps you grow a heart full of love and care for everyone, including yourself. It's a beautiful way to spread kindness in the world.

The Essence of Metta Meditation

Metta meditation is like growing a garden of love in your heart. It's about learning to love not just your friends and family, but also yourself and even people you might not know very well. Imagine your heart is like a garden. In this garden, you plant seeds of love, kindness, and good wishes. You start by planting these seeds for yourself, wishing yourself happiness, peace, and love. Then, you water these seeds and watch them grow. Next, you extend these good wishes to people you care about, like your friends and family. It's like sharing your beautiful garden with them. But Metta meditation doesn't stop there. You keep extending your good wishes to people you don't know so well, like acquaintances or even people you might have had disagreements with. You're like a generous gardener, sharing the beauty of your garden with everyone. And finally, you send these warm-hearted wishes to everyone in the world, even to those you may have never met. Your garden of love becomes boundless, like the sky. The essence of Metta meditation is about growing love and kindness in your heart, not just for a few people, but for everyone and even for yourself. It's like turning your heart into a garden of love that keeps growing and spreading its beauty to the whole world.

Historical Origins

Metta meditation has a long history, like a beautiful old tree with deep roots. It comes from Buddhism, which is an ancient tradition. But the cool thing is, this meditation isn't just for Buddhists. It's like a tasty dish that people from all over the world can enjoy. So, way back when, in the teachings of Buddha, they talked about this loving-kindness stuff. They believed that practicing Metta could bring a lot of peace and happiness inside us. It's like a magic potion for the heart! As time went on, people from different backgrounds and beliefs started to see the value in Metta meditation. They realized that it's not tied to just one religion; it's a practice that anyone can use to bring more love and kindness into their lives. So, you can think of Metta meditation as a timeless practice that has been passed down through generations, like a precious gem that everyone can treasure.

Techniques and Practice

Metta meditation typically follows a structured pattern that progresses from self-compassion to extending loving-kindness outward. Here's a general overview of the practice:

- **Begin with Yourself**: So, imagine you're finding a cozy spot where you won't be disturbed. You close your eyes and take some nice, deep breaths to calm down and get in the zone. It's like your own little peaceful bubble. You start saying kind and loving things to yourself in your mind. It's like giving yourself a pep talk filled with warmth. You might say something like, *"I wish for myself to be happy, healthy, and live with ease."* It's like sending yourself good vibes and well wishes. You deserve that, right? This part is all about being your own best friend and treating yourself with lots of love and care. After all, you're pretty awesome!

- **Loved Ones**: After you've given yourself some loving kindness, it's time to spread that warmth to the people you care about – your loved ones, friends, or family. You start by thinking about someone close to your heart, maybe a family member or a dear friend. Then, in your mind, you say something like, *"I wish for [their name] to be happy, healthy, and live with ease."* It's like you're sending out good vibes and well wishes to them. This part is like sharing your positive energy and love with the people who mean a lot to you. You're like a kind-hearted messenger of happiness and good health!

- **Neutral Individuals**: After sending love to yourself and your loved ones, you expand your loving-kindness circle even wider. Think about people you might not know very well, like acquaintances or even strangers you've seen around. Picture them in your mind, and send them those kind thoughts and wishes, just like you did for yourself and your loved ones. You're like a spreading wave of goodwill, making the circle of love bigger and bigger. This part of Metta meditation helps you see the connection you have with everyone, even people you don't know so well. It's like sending out ripples of kindness into the world!.

- **Difficult Individuals**: In Metta meditation, you take a step further by sending loving-kindness to people who might be a bit challenging for you. These could be folks you've had disagreements with or maybe don't get along with so well. It might seem a little tricky, but it's a way to soften any hard feelings and find common ground. You're essentially saying, "Even though we may have our differences, I still wish you happiness, health, and ease in life." It's a bit like mending fences and letting go of negativity. By doing this, you're chipping away at the walls that separate you from others, promoting understanding, and making room for more love and compassion in your heart..

- **All Beings**: In Metta meditation, the last step is like *the grand finale*. After sending loving-kindness to yourself, loved ones, neutral folks, and even the challenging ones, you're ready for the big moment. You take a deep breath and imagine sending your warm, kind feelings out into the world, far and wide. You don't pick and choose anymore; you're spreading love and well-wishes to every living being. It's like your heart is a big, glowing ball of love, and you're sharing it with all creatures on Earth. You're saying, *"May every being, no matter who they are, be happy, healthy, and live with ease."* This step reminds you of the deep connection we all share, like we're part of one big family on this planet. It's a beautiful way to wrap up your Metta meditation practice, leaving you with a heart full of love and compassion for everyone.

Impact of Metta

Metta meditation offers numerous benefits that complement and enrich mindfulness practice:

- **Cultivation of Compassion**: Metta meditation is like planting seeds of compassion in your heart, and with each session, these seeds grow into beautiful, blooming flowers of kindness. It starts with you, as you shower yourself with warm, caring thoughts and wishes. Then, you let this kindness flow outwards. You think of people you love, folks you don't really know, and even those who might be a bit tricky to get along with. With each thought and wish, your heart expands. You start to feel a deep connection with everyone around you, like you're all part of a big, loving family. You genuinely want everyone to be happy, healthy, and free from suffering. This practice turns you into a compassionate being. You become more understanding, patient, and willing to lend a helping hand.

- **Emotional Regulation**: When you practice Metta, you're like a superhero who can regulate their emotions with ease. It's like having a secret power that helps you stay calm and compassionate even when things get tough. Here's how it works: By generating those warm, fuzzy feelings of love and kindness during Metta meditation, you strengthen your emotional muscles. It's like doing push-ups for your heart and mind. So, when challenges and difficulties come your way, you're ready. You don't get overwhelmed by anger, frustration, or stress. Instead, you respond with a heart full of compassion and understanding. It's like having a shield of kindness that protects you from emotional storms. Metta meditation becomes your emotional refuge, your safe place. It's where you recharge your emotional superpowers, so you can face life's challenges with a heart full of love and resilience.

- **Interconnectedness**: Imagine you're holding a beautiful, sparkling thread. This thread represents Metta, the loving-kindness you cultivate in your heart during meditation. Now, imagine that this thread doesn't just connect you to one person or a few people. It stretches out endlessly, like a web that connects you to everyone and everything in the world. This is what Metta meditation teaches you – the idea that we're all connected, like a big, intricate web of life. It's like realizing that you and the person on the other side of the world, or even a tiny ant crawling on the ground, are all part of the same beautiful tapestry of existence. This understanding of interconnectedness is like a gentle breeze that blows away the fog of separateness. It helps you see that we're all in this together, like members of a big, diverse family. So, when you practice Metta, you're not just sending love and kindness to one person; you're sending it out to the whole world, to every living being. It's a powerful reminder that we're all part of the same grand adventure called life.

- **Healing Relationships**: Imagine you have a garden of beautiful flowers, but over time, some of the flowers have withered, and the garden doesn't look as lovely as it once did. These withered flowers represent relationships that have become strained or hurt. Now, imagine that you have a magical watering can filled with Metta, that loving-kindness we've been talking about. When you sprinkle this Metta on those withered relationships, it's like giving them a special kind of water that helps them bloom again. The resentments and hurt feelings in those relationships start to soften, just like the soil in your garden becomes more nourishing. Slowly but surely, the flowers of those relationships begin to grow again, becoming more beautiful and vibrant than before. Metta meditation has this amazing power to mend the bonds between people, to heal the wounds, and to create an atmosphere of love and kindness. It's like a gentle rain that brings life back to your garden of relationships, making it flourish with happiness and understanding.

Metta meditation is a radiant pathway that intertwines mindfulness with boundless compassion. Through the cultivation of loving-kindness, we not only transform our relationship with ourselves but also with the world around us. This practice has the power to dissolve barriers, ignite empathy, and foster a profound sense of interconnectedness. Metta meditation is like a beautiful path that combines mindfulness with boundless compassion. It's like a magic spell that breaks down walls and makes us understand and care about others more. When we practice Metta meditation regularly, it's like watering a plant. Our hearts grow and become more loving, and our connection with all living things deepens. This can make our lives happier and more meaningful. It also helps us become emotionally stronger and see the bright side of life. As you keep practicing Metta meditation, you're not just improving your mindfulness, but you're also making your heart shine with love, kindness, and a warm feeling of goodwill towards all. It's a beautiful journey that touches your very soul.

CHAPTER - VI

Mindfulness and Beyond

Mindfulness and Spirituality

The practice of mindfulness has ancient and diverse origins that span cultures, religions, and philosophies. From its roots in Eastern spiritual traditions to its integration into modern psychology, mindfulness has evolved over millennia. Exploring the historical roots of mindfulness offers insight into its rich tapestry and provides a context for understanding its relevance in contemporary life. In Hinduism and Buddhism, mindfulness is an essential component of spiritual practices like meditation, leading to greater awareness, inner peace, and enlightenment.

Hinduism is a complex and diverse religion that has a long history of incorporating mindfulness practices into its spiritual traditions. At the heart of Hinduism is the idea of achieving moksha, or liberation from the cycle of rebirth and suffering. One way to achieve this state of enlightenment is through the practice of mindfulness.

In Hinduism, mindfulness is often cultivated through meditation and the practice of yoga. These practices are designed to quiet the mind and cultivate a sense of inner peace and awareness. The ultimate goal of mindfulness in Hinduism is to achieve a state of samadhi, or deep concentration, where the individual experiences a sense of oneness with the universe.

Hinduism also talks a lot about something called "karma," which means that the things you do have consequences, either good or bad. When people practice mindfulness, they become more aware of what they do and how it affects themselves and others. This can lead to good karma, which is like a good outcome or result. So, mindfulness in Hinduism is not just about feeling good; it's also about doing good things and making the world a better place.

Buddhism is a spiritual tradition that places a strong emphasis on mindfulness and the cultivation of awareness. At the heart of Buddhism is the idea of the Four Noble Truths, which state that suffering is an inherent part of life, but that it is possible to overcome suffering through mindfulness and the cultivation of wisdom.

In the rich tapestry of Buddhism, mindfulness is not merely a practice; it is a way of life deeply woven into its core teachings. The cultivation of mindfulness finds its essence in meditation and the profound exploration of the Four Foundations of Mindfulness. These foundations serve as pillars, supporting individuals in their journey towards a heightened awareness of the self and the world around them. They encompass mindfulness of the body, feelings, mind, and phenomena, each offering a unique perspective on existence.

In the words of the *Dalai Lama, "Mindfulness is the gatekeeper to tranquility."* This gatekeeper role is evident in the first foundation, mindfulness of the body. Through this practice, individuals delve into the intricate dance of sensations, acknowledging impermanence, and recognizing that the body is in a perpetual state of flux. This realization, deeply rooted in Buddhist philosophy, allows individuals to develop a sense of detachment from the ever-changing physical form, fostering a profound sense of inner peace.

The second foundation, mindfulness of feelings, goes hand in hand with the Dalai Lama's wisdom: *"The ultimate source of happiness is not money and power, but warm-heartedness."* It encourages individuals to discern the ebb and flow of emotions, understanding that feelings, like passing clouds, come and go. By observing these emotions with a compassionate heart, individuals can lessen their attachment to them, paving the way for a heart warmed by kindness and free from the chains of attachment.

In the third foundation, mindfulness of the mind, we find the wisdom of the *Dalai Lama* resonating: *"Our prime purpose in this life is to help others."* Through this practice, individuals delve into the depths of their consciousness, acknowledging the ceaseless stream of thoughts and emotions. By embracing the impermanent nature of the mind, they learn to let go of rigid attachments to thoughts, freeing themselves from unnecessary suffering.

The fourth foundation, mindfulness of phenomena, invites individuals to explore the intricate web of interconnectedness. It aligns with the *Dalai Lama's* insight that *"we are all interconnected; all beings are part of the same journey of awakening."* By recognizing the interdependence of all things, individuals cultivate a sense of unity with the universe, reducing their attachment to the illusion of separateness.

Mindfulness in Buddhism is a profound journey of self-discovery and liberation. It is not about clinging to the transient but about embracing impermanence, fostering inner peace, and spreading compassion. As the *Dalai Lama* reminds us, *"This is my simple religion: There is no need for temples; no need for complicated philosophy. Our own brain, our own heart is our temple; the philosophy is kindness."* Mindfulness in Buddhism is the path to that temple of kindness and wisdom, a path illuminated by the timeless teachings of the Buddha and echoed in the words of great spiritual leaders like the *Dalai Lama.*

For example, the practice of mindfulness can help individuals become more empathetic and understanding of others' perspectives, leading to better communication and more harmonious relationships. Mindfulness can also improve work productivity and performance by increasing focus, attention, and creativity.

Mindfulness is like a special tool that can help people in many ways, including finding more meaning and purpose in life. When you practice mindfulness along with spirituality, it's like a double benefit. It can help you in many ways. First, it can make you feel like your life has more meaning and purpose. You become more aware of what you think and do, and this helps you understand what really matters to you. So, you start making choices that make you feel happier and more satisfied with your life. Second, it's like a tool for personal growth. It helps you become a better person, not just for yourself but for the people around you too. You become more understanding and kind. And when more people practice mindfulness this way, it's like a ripple effect. It can make the whole community better. People understand each other more, show more compassion, and everyone's well-being gets a boost.

Mindfulness and spirituality are like a delicious blend of peanut butter and jelly. They complement each other so well that it's almost like they were made for each other. Remember what *Lao Tzu* said: *"When I let go of what I am, I become what I might be."* That's the magic of this blend - it opens doors you never knew existed. When you see a group of monks sitting cross-legged in a monastery, practicing mindfulness meditation, they're not just emptying their minds; they're filling their hearts with the wisdom of spirituality. As they breathe in, they connect with the universe. As they breathe out, they find inner peace. Imagine a world where everyone practices mindfulness with spirituality. People stop and listen to each other, compassion flows like a river, and understanding becomes the norm. It's not just about inner peace; it's about making the world a better place, one mindful step at a time.

Mindfulness and Creativity

Mindfulness can have a profound impact on creativity, helping individuals tap into their inner resources and unleash their creative potential. By cultivating mindfulness, individuals can overcome creative blocks, access deeper levels of creativity, and develop greater clarity and focus in their work. At its core, creativity involves the ability to generate new ideas and insights by connecting seemingly unrelated concepts or experiences. However, this process can be hindered by distractions, self-doubt, and a lack of focus. By practicing mindfulness, individuals can overcome these obstacles and tap into their innate creativity.

Think of your mind as a canvas where creativity can bloom. When you practice mindfulness, it's like you've laid the perfect foundation – a serene, distraction-free canvas. This allows your creative thoughts to shine, unburdened by the clutter of worries and distractions. Mindfulness tunes your senses to the world's symphony. When you're fully present, your senses become your allies. You see colors more vividly, feel textures more deeply, and hear melodies in everyday sounds. This heightened sensory awareness is a treasure trove of inspiration for creative minds. Ever had a brilliant idea pop into your head during a moment of stillness? That's mindfulness at work. By calming the mind's chatter, mindfulness lets your creative thoughts emerge like stars in a dark sky. It's like having a spotlight on your ideas, making them shine even brighter. Creativity can be a tricky beast. It sometimes hides in the corners of your mind, waiting to be discovered. Mindfulness acts as a bridge, connecting you to those hidden creative nooks. You'll find solutions to problems you thought were unsolvable and connect the dots in ways you never imagined. Creative blocks are like mental roadblocks that stop your ideas from flowing. Mindfulness bulldozes these blocks. When you're mindful, you become an idea generator, a thought explorer, and a creative problem-solver. You'll see that there are no roadblocks—only stepping stones to your creative paradise. Remember that mindfulness isn't just for artists. Whether you're a scientist, a writer, a chef, or an accountant, mindfulness can infuse your work with fresh perspectives and innovative ideas. It's like adding a pinch of magic to your everyday tasks..

In addition to enhancing the creative process itself, mindfulness can also help individuals overcome the stress and anxiety that often accompany creative pursuits. By cultivating mindfulness, individuals can develop greater resilience and emotional regulation, allowing them to better cope with the ups and downs of the creative process. This can lead to a greater sense of well-being and fulfillment in both the creative process and life in general. By doing so, individuals can connect with their inner resources and unleash their creative potential in new and exciting ways.

An important view to consider is the role of mindfulness in promoting self-compassion and self-acceptance. In the process of personal growth, individuals may often encounter their own limitations and shortcomings, which can lead to feelings of self-doubt and self-criticism. By cultivating mindfulness, individuals can learn to approach their own experiences with kindness and compassion, recognizing that struggles and setbacks are a natural part of the human experience.

Mindfulness can also promote a sense of interconnectedness and unity with others, leading to a greater sense of meaning and purpose in life. By cultivating mindfulness, individuals can develop a deeper appreciation for the present moment and the people and experiences that make it meaningful.

Finally, it is important to note that mindfulness is not a panacea for all of life's challenges. While it can be a powerful tool for personal growth and development, it is not a substitute for professional help when needed. If individuals are struggling with mental health issues, it is important to seek out the appropriate support and resources.

In conclusion, mindfulness can be a valuable tool for personal growth and development, promoting self-awareness, emotional regulation, and overall well-being. By cultivating mindfulness, individuals can develop a greater sense of compassion and acceptance towards themselves and others, leading to more fulfilling and meaningful lives. While mindfulness is not a cure-all, it can be a powerful supplement to other forms of therapy and support.

Mindfulness and Social Growth

Mindfulness is a universal practice that transcends borders and cultures, offering a path to personal growth, spiritual development, and social betterment for all. From ancient wisdom to modern relevance, mindfulness is a practice that unites people across the globe.

One way mindfulness can promote social growth is by fostering greater awareness of societal issues. It's akin to opening our eyes to the world's intricacies. Mindfulness sharpens our perception, allowing us to notice nuances we might have previously overlooked. We become attuned to the struggles and injustices faced by others. This heightened awareness serves as the first step towards effecting change.

Mindfulness doesn't stop at mere awareness; it also cultivates empathy. It allows us to step into the shoes of others, genuinely understanding their experiences. Empathy isn't passive; it's a catalyst for transformation. Mindfulness awakens a sense of responsibility within us, empowering us to make a difference, even through small acts of kindness.

Social growth doesn't always necessitate grand movements; mindfulness teaches us that small, everyday actions can create profound ripples of positive change. A compassionate community thrives on these small acts of kindness, fostering unity and support. Mindfulness isn't just a personal journey; it's a global one.

Beyond empathy and compassion, mindfulness fuels social engagement and action. It's not just about recognizing issues; it's about transforming awareness into meaningful deeds. Mindfulness emboldens us to be vocal advocates for those whose voices often go unheard. It amplifies our actions, turning them into waves of positive change.

Creating positive change is akin to creating ripples in a pond. Mindfulness has the power to amplify these ripples into waves of transformation. With mindfulness, we engage in actions that lead to positive change with a calm and clear mind. It fosters a sense of community where shared values drive meaningful improvements.

Moreover, mindfulness promotes self-care and resilience among individuals working towards positive change. It equips them with emotional resilience, helping them navigate the challenges and intense emotions that often accompany their efforts. Mindfulness acts as a guide in the midst of change, leading individuals to self-awareness, setting limits, and emphasizing the importance of self-renewal.

Avoiding burnout is crucial for those dedicated to making positive changes, and mindfulness introduces the concept of the mindful pause. This pause allows individuals to take breaks without guilt, ensuring they remain effective and energized in their pursuit of positive change. Ultimately, mindfulness creates a harmonious balance, ensuring that change-makers not only work towards a better world but also take care of themselves.

In conclusion, mindfulness is a global tool for social growth. It enhances awareness, empathy, and engagement with social issues, contributing to a more equitable and just world. However, lasting change requires both mindfulness and systemic efforts. With a deep commitment to mindfulness and social justice, the world can become a more compassionate and equitable place for everyone.

CHAPTER – VII

Alas, In Nutshell

Mindfulness is a profound practice that enriches every aspect of our lives, from our relationship with ourselves to our connections with others. In the midst of our frantic, tech-driven lives, where we juggle tasks and remain tethered to screens, mindfulness emerges as a timeless remedy. It's not a passing trend but a profound practice, inviting us to be fully present, non-judgmental, and open-hearted in every moment. Originating in ancient Eastern traditions, mindfulness has transcended boundaries, becoming a universal practice. It's not about escaping the mundane but about awakening to each moment's richness, like a curious cat exploring a cardboard box.

Through mindfulness, we learn to cultivate self-compassion, regulate our emotions, and develop a deep understanding of our thoughts and feelings. This practice equips us with the tools to navigate life's challenges gracefully, promoting resilience and mental clarity. In the realm of relationships, mindfulness acts as a bridge that connects individuals on a profound level. It fosters empathy, deepens connections, and allows us to be fully present with our loved ones. Like a well-tended garden, our relationships thrive when nurtured with presence, effective communication, and emotional regulation.

The journey of mindfulness is transformative, like planting seeds in the garden of our lives. As we tend to these seeds, they grow, not only strengthening our connection with ourselves but also enriching our bonds with others. It's an adventure we embark on together, evolving as individuals and as partners. Just like a beautifully woven tapestry, mindfulness stitches authenticity, compassion, and mutual commitment into the fabric of our relationships. Love is the thread that binds it all together, and each mindful moment contributes to this exquisite creation.

Recap of the benefits of mindfulness

In this book, we've explored mindfulness benefits in various areas of life. To recap:

1. Mindfulness enhances mental health, aiding self-awareness and emotional regulation, reducing stress, anxiety, and depression, and fostering resilience.
2. It boosts cognitive abilities, improving creativity, problem-solving, and idea generation, especially in creative pursuits.
3. Mindfulness fosters social connectedness, empathy, and compassion, improving relationships and promoting engagement in positive social and political change.
4. It fuels personal growth and spiritual development, enhancing self-awareness and acceptance for greater fulfillment.
5. Mindfulness supports physical health by reducing stress, lowering blood pressure, easing chronic pain, and strengthening the immune system.

It is important to note that the benefits of mindfulness are not limited to these domains alone. Mindfulness has been shown to have a wide range of positive effects on various aspects of our lives. While the practice of mindfulness may take time and effort to cultivate, the benefits are well worth the investment.

In addition to the benefits, we have discussed in this chapter, here are some additional benefits of mindfulness that we have covered in previous discussions:

- Improved focus and attention: Mindfulness can improve our ability to concentrate and stay focused, making us more productive and efficient in our work and daily activities.

- Better decision-making: By cultivating mindfulness, we can develop greater clarity of thought and decision-making ability, allowing us to make more informed and effective choices.

- Enhanced creativity: In addition to the benefits, we discussed in the chapter on mindfulness and creativity, mindfulness can also enhance our ability to think outside the box and generate innovative ideas.

- Reduced rumination: Mindfulness can help us break the cycle of negative and repetitive thoughts, reducing feelings of anxiety and depression.

- Increased resilience: Mindfulness can promote greater resilience, allowing us to bounce back from setbacks and challenges more easily.

- Improved sleep: By reducing stress and promoting relaxation, mindfulness can improve the quality of our sleep, leading to greater energy and vitality during waking hours.

- Enhanced relationships: Mindfulness can promote greater empathy, understanding, and communication in our relationships, leading to greater harmony and connection with others.

- Improved self-esteem: Mindfulness can help us develop a more positive self-image and increase our self-esteem, which can improve our overall well-being and lead to greater success in our personal and professional lives.

- Reduced physical symptoms of stress: Mindfulness has been shown to reduce physical symptoms of stress, such as headaches, muscle tension, and digestive issues, which can improve our overall physical health.

- Increased emotional intelligence: Mindfulness can help us become more aware of our own emotions and the emotions of others, which can increase our emotional intelligence and improve our social interactions.

- Improved immune function: Studies have shown that mindfulness can boost our immune function, which can help us fight off illness and disease.

- Greater sense of purpose: Mindfulness can help us gain a greater sense of purpose and meaning in life, which can improve our overall sense of well-being and fulfillment.

Overall, the benefits of mindfulness are wide-ranging and can improve many aspects of our lives. By practicing mindfulness regularly, we can develop greater self-awareness, emotional regulation, and empathy towards others, as well as enhance our cognitive abilities, creativity, and physical health. Whether we are seeking personal growth, social change, or simply a greater sense of well-being, mindfulness can be a valuable tool to help us achieve our goals.

Final thoughts on Integrating Mindfulness Into Daily Life

Throughout this book, we've explored the multifaceted benefits of mindfulness for our physical, mental, emotional well-being, relationships, and productivity. Now, let's delve into the practical steps of seamlessly integrating mindfulness into our daily lives to harness these advantages.

The initial step is making mindfulness a top priority. Dedicate time each day for mindfulness practices, such as meditation, deep breathing, or simply immersing yourself in the present moment. Establishing a routine, whether it's morning or bedtime mindfulness, fosters consistency.

Moreover, weaving mindfulness into routine activities is essential. Transform mundane moments into mindful ones; relish each bite during meals with mindful eating or engage in mindful walking by connecting with every step's sensations. By infusing mindfulness into these everyday rituals, you nurture heightened presence and awareness.

Surrounding yourself with like-minded individuals who value mindfulness is another key aspect. Consider joining a mindfulness community or attending a retreat. The presence of fellow mindfulness practitioners can inspire and motivate your own journey.

Integrating mindfulness extends beyond formal practice. Mindful interactions with others are equally crucial. Engage in mindful communication by listening deeply and being fully present during conversations. This enriches relationships and strengthens your ability to connect authentically.

Remember that mindfulness isn't a quick fix; it's a lifelong commitment. As life throws challenges your way, mindfulness serves as your reliable tool to stay grounded, composed, and focused.

Approach mindfulness with curiosity and openness. Rather than judging your thoughts or emotions, observe them with a non-judgmental attitude and nurture self-compassion. Embrace yourself as you are to cultivate self-awareness and foster positive relationships with yourself and others.

In conclusion, integrating mindfulness into your daily life yields an array of benefits across physical, mental, and emotional well-being. By prioritizing mindfulness, incorporating it into routine activities, and approaching it with curiosity and openness, you can nurture greater presence, awareness, and resilience. With unwavering dedication, this lifelong mindfulness practice equips you to gracefully navigate life's ups and downs.

Acknowledgement

With reverence and gratitude, I dedicate this work to my
Eternal Teacher
"Sri Guru"
Sri Gurubhyo Namah

References

Allard, S. (2019, 5 19). *Buddhist mindfulness is all the rage, but Hinduism has a deep meditation tradition too.* From hinduamerican: https://www.hinduamerican.org/blog/buddhist-mindfulness-is-all-the-rage-but-hinduism-has-a-deep-meditation-tradition-too

The Dalai Lama on Why Leaders Should Be Mindful, Selfless, and Compassionate. (2019, 2 20). From Harvard Business Review: https://hbr.org/2019/02/the-dalai-lama-on-why-leaders-should-be-mindful-selfless-and-compassionate

Davis, D. M. (2012, 8). *What are the benefits of mindfulness.* From American Psychological Association: https://www.apa.org/monitor/2012/07-08/ce-corner

DISCREMENTSPIRIT. (2023, 1 14). *Meditation and Mindfulness.* From timesofindia: https://timesofindia.indiatimes.com/readersblog/discrenmentspirit/meditation-and-mindfulness-49213/

discrenmentspirit. (2023, 1 14). *Meditation and Mindfulness.* From timesofindia: https://timesofindia.indiatimes.com/readersblog/discrenmentspirit/meditation-and-mindfulness-49213/

Grabowski, S. (2023, 5 30). *The Ultimate Guide to Metta Meditation.* From themindfulsteward: https://themindfulsteward.com/the-ultimate-guide-to-metta-meditation/

How to Practice Gratitude. (n.d.). From mindful: https://www.mindful.org/an-introduction-to-mindful-gratitude/

Kapoor, M. (2023, 5 4). *Mindfulness: A journey to the present moment.* From timesofindia: https://timesofindia.indiatimes.com/readersblog/thoughts-aloud/mindfulness-a-journey-to-the-present-moment-53390/

Lama, D. (n.d.). *The Path to Tranquility.*

Meditation. (n.d.). From wikipedia: https://en.wikipedia.org/wiki/Meditation

Mindfulness. (n.d.). From livinglifefully: https://www.livinglifefully.com/mindfulness.htm

Mindfulness. (n.d.). From wikipedia: https://en.wikipedia.org/wiki/Mindfulness#:~:text=In%20a%20Buddhist%20context%20the,causation%20and%20other%20Buddhist%20teachings.

My religion is very simple. My religion is kindness. (n.d.). From quotespedia: https://www.quotespedia.org/authors/d/dalai-lama/my-religion-is-very-simple-my-religion-is-kindness-dalai-lama/

Naithani, R. (n.d.). *Mindfulness: The power of being 'here and now'.* From peoplematters: https://www.peoplematters.in/article/diversity/legal-hr-can-you-fire-a-pregnant-woman-employee-16945

Nash, J. (2019, 7 27). *What Is Loving-Kindness Meditation.* From positivepsychology: https://positivepsychology.com/loving-kindness-meditation/

Picard, C. (2017, 215). *The Origins, Principles and Practices of Insight Mediation.* https://revistademediacion.com/en/articulos/the-origins-principles-and-practices-of-insight-mediation/index.html#:~:text=The%20process%20of%20Insight%20mediation,possibilities%20and%205)%20make%20decisions.

Reid, S. (n.d.). *Gratitude: The Benefits and How to Practice It.* From helpguide: https://www.helpguide.org/articles/mental-health/gratitude.htm

Sasson, R. (n.d.). *Creative Visualization vs Affirmations—What's the Difference?* From Success Consciousness: https://www.successconsciousness.com/blog/creative-visualization/creative-visualization-vs-affirmations/

Saxena, S. (2022, 7 19). *How to Practice Gratitude.* From choosingtherapy: https://www.choosingtherapy.com/how-to-practice-gratitude/

Swan, D. (2023, 8 31). *10 Visualization Techniques to Achieve Your Goals.* From clickup: https://clickup.com/blog/visualization-techniques/

Tolle, E. (n.d.). A New Earth: Awakening to Your Life's Purpose. In E. Tolle.

visualization and affirmation. (n.d.). From selfpause: https://selfpause.com/visualization/visualization-and-affirmation-powerful-tools-for-achieving-your-goals/

(n.d.). From NMVVRC: https://www.nmvvrc.org/media/ozigtswy/mindfulness-and-meditation.pdf

(n.d.). From issuu: https://issuu.com/junctionmag/docs/junction_february_22